For my mother and father,
Karolina and Jan Kanik

Keep your thoughts positive,
because your thoughts become your words.
Keep your words positive,
because your words become your behavior.
Keep your behavior positive,
because your behavior become your habits.
Keep your habits positive,
because your habits become your values.
Keep your values positive,
because your values become your destiny.

—Mahatma Gandhi

CONTENTS

DEDICATION iii
GANDHI QUOTE v
PREFACE ix
CHAPTER 1   Grace Is Back 1
CHAPTER 2   A New Way of Pursuing Happiness:
                     Epigenetics, Heart Unity, and Mysticism 9
CHAPTER 3   New Physics: Mystical links between Science
                     and New Reality 25
CHAPTER 4   My Mother's Eyes: An Encounter with the Mystical 39
CHAPTER 5   Relationships and Perceptions:
                     Conversation with a Monk 51
CHAPTER 6   Modern Mysticism in Therapy 61
CHAPTER 7   Overcoming Adversity 75
CHAPTER 8   Ancient Wisdom Connection: Aristotle on Happiness 85
CHAPTER 9   My Father's Suicide: An encounter with
                     Dark Mysticism 93
CHAPTER 10 Peter: Conversation with a Professor of Theology 109
CHAPTER 11 ALEX: Conversation with a Professor of Psychology 115
CHAPTER 12 How I Met My Wife: Creating and
                     Preserving Lasting Relationships 121
CHAPTER 13 Closing the Circle 131
NEW BEGINNINGS 143
ACKNOWLEDGEMENTS 145

PREFACE

I am. Everything that exists, everything that ever was, and everything that ever will be is contained in these two words. *I am*—more commonly known as God. Everything that follows after "I am" is therefore a self-fulfilling prophecy: I am happy, I am healthy, I am prosperous, I am kind, I am a Modern Mystic! Each and every one of us is an essential part of the divine intervention, an intentional creation imbued with meaning. In fact, we are entities that make the self-aware universe possible. There are no mistakes or accidents, we are all here for each other; without each other, we could not exist. The very fact that we humans do exist—with such astonishing potential that we're only beginning to discover—is an amazing phenomenon that is nothing short of mystical!

If you ever feel that life and the world are irrational, don't be alarmed, that is the human condition; it is precisely because we are continuously attempting to reconcile what is really real with the perceptions of our minds. We could tap the deep reality and beauty of our own inner universe, and sometimes we do—through reflections, prayer, or meditations. However, too often these moments of peace and sanity are squashed by our "rational" mind that is working overtime suppressing the wisdom of our hearts to pursue what appears to be practical and sensible.

"Mysticism" is another word that can be perplexing to some and no wonder: the very subject implies the unknown, the mystical.

Let me offer some definitions:

1. Wikipedia describes mysticism as: "A constellation of distinctive practices, discourses, texts, institutions, traditions, and experiences aimed at human transformation, variously defined in different traditions."
2. Albert Schweitzer offered, "Any profound view of the universe is mystic in that it brings men into spiritual relationship with the Infinite. ... Rational thinking, if it goes deep, ends of necessity in the irrational realm of mysticism. It has, of course, to deal with life and the world, both of which are nonrational entities."
3. Albert Einstein said, "The finest emotion of which we are capable is the mystic emotion. ... Anyone to whom this feeling is alien, who is no longer capable of wonderment and lives in a state of fear is a dead man. To know that what is impenetrable for us really exists and manifests itself as the highest wisdom and the most radiant beauty, whose gross forms alone are intelligible to our poor faculties—this knowledge, this feeling ... is the core of the true religious sentiment."
4. Christian mystic St. Theresa intoned, "Mysticism is a belief that union with or absorption into the Deity or the absolute, or the spiritual apprehension of knowledge inaccessible to the intellect, may be attained through contemplation and self-surrender."

Some people believe that mystics are born, that they have a natural "talent" and don't follow any particular dogma. It seems that mysticism is an impulse or a kind of intuition that drives the mystic to live a faithful or virtuous life. But what about the rest of us? It is generally accepted that we are all capable of knowing the difference between right and wrong, that we all "know the score." We know that it is our nature to only be happy when we are compassionate and contributing, which in turn leads us toward self-actualization. We know that helping others gives us feelings of self-worth and inner satisfaction. We know that if we choose to engage in destructive emotions, such as hate, domination, persecution, or acts of terror against our fellow man, it leaves us in internal emotional and psychological disarray. Then what exactly is a mystic?

The mystic is driven to know, to create, to teach, and to learn. Mystics are naturally flexible and open to new points of view, an attitude that allows them to learn more about themselves, others, and their environment. The mystic is characterized by pursuing progress toward a worthy idea. The goal might be raising a family, aligning with their life purpose through their career, or forming and engaging in lasting, meaningful relationships. Mystics are interested in truth; therefore, they seek connection with their souls—the source of truth. They practice not only by reflection and quiet contemplation, but also by diligently executing their professions or contributing toward their relationships with dedication that often extends beyond their own comfort.

If this sounds familiar, that's because it is. We are all mystics! We all come from the same divine source. We're just too distracted to see it. We are immersed in a reality that we impose on ourselves by focusing on what we perceive to be important. Sometimes we stray from the divine path, and that often results in anxieties and emotional chaos. Sometimes we cope by medicating the symptoms to silence our confused minds. The remedy however, is much simpler: When we connect our hearts with our souls, our minds will follow suit. This knowledge has been somehow neglected over the millennia. Fortunately, it is easily recovered through deep reflection during our contemplation, or by seeking the assistance of a professional counselor who can help guide us back to our natural state of being.

This book is designed to raise the reader's awareness; it is a reminder that our world is teeming with the mystical, as is the whole of the known universe. When we get caught up in the rush of everyday living, we tend to miss the opportunity to stop and enjoy our lives, to live in the moment.

Instead we tend to carry on with our multitasking until something goes wrong. Then perhaps we seek help in therapy. This provides an opportunity to slow down and reflect on what is really going on in our lives and helps us redirect our focus on what really matters. What does matter? The unification of the mind, body, and spirit into a cohesive whole is what seems to matter. However, if this just sounds like another attempt to tap into so-called "spirituality," you will be relieved to hear that thanks to recent discoveries within the realm of the New Physics, the line between science and mysticism is blurring. Within these pages, we will explore this tentative meeting of the minds.

I offer this book as reinforcement of the importance of reconnecting with ourselves and others to rediscover meaning, passion, and a sense of wonder—the state of the mystical.

***

I came to write this following my encounter with the mystical in the context of therapy sessions with my clients. My first realization about the phenomenon came while I was still at university. I volunteered as a facilitator in groups of men who were battling or recovering from addiction. For me, it was a revelation to observe that at a certain point during the group discussions, there was an exchange of some kind of energy in the room between the participants and the facilitator. To allow this energy to flourish, I quickly learned that my role was to simply observe rather than lead the group. Through this technique, I was physically present while being somehow withdrawn from my body as if I was hovering above the group session and observing this incredible connection between the participants.

After graduation, I began working with refugees seeking asylum from their war-torn countries; I served as a torture and trauma counselor. It was difficult to hear their horrific stories, and the only way I could communicate was through an interpreter. I quickly realized that the counseling skills I had so diligently studied at university were of no use. These clients had no concept of "counseling"; where they came from the idea of professional therapy was nonexistent, so they largely didn't understand what my role was. Many of my clients from Africa or the Middle East were accustomed to seeking resolution to their problems by consulting their local village chief, shaman, or spiritual leader. For them, confiding their deepest, most profound secrets to a stranger outside their cultural circles was simply inconceivable. Here I was:

a person who looked different, spoke a foreign tongue, and worse, was perceived as an authority figure. At this point, I decided that if I were going to be able to form any kind of meaningful therapeutic alliance with them, I would have to expand—or even invent—some therapeutic strategies beyond those I learned at university. Fortunately, my interest in energy fields, quantum physics, and the canon of ancient wisdom literature combined to enable me to look at therapy from a different angle. I trusted my intuition and allowed the newly discovered energy to flow. I was astonished by the instant results. Suddenly, I realized that out of necessity, I had stumbled on innovative ways of eliciting therapeutic communication. My excitement was immense. I decided to test my theories further ...

As my career was unfolding, I focused on this mystical energy flow in my counseling room. Interestingly, I noticed that during my collaboration with clients of all kinds, the same principals of this energy flow applied.

As I continued my investigation, I determined to perform more structured scholarly research on the topic, and that led me to writing my master's dissertation on the subject of mysticism as a therapeutic tool. While I was curious about this phenomenon, I didn't invent anything—I only stumbled on the healing potential of mysticism. I wondered whether any of my professional colleagues had documented this mystical turn, and was not terribly surprised to discover that they had, indeed! My ongoing exploration culminated in the book you're now reading.

The central premise is that mysticism takes many forms, and it occurs in our lives more often than we realize.

Herein you will read profiles of childhood struggles and ways to overcome them. The stories are examples that illustrate the different faces of mysticism; some are linked to explanations about the flow of mystical energy observed during sessions in the counseling room. The description of a hypnotic trance related in Chapter 4 takes the reader into a different realm of the mystical journey, and while it is somewhat unusual, it can be experienced by anyone.

Other stories revolve around the field of New Science and its discoveries. There are also descriptions linked with examples of strange and mystical phenomena from the world of quantum physics, as well as the nature of perceptions from a holographic universe. More on the subject of perception is revealed in Chapter 5, Relationships and Perceptions: Conversation with a monk.

There is also a fictionalized interaction between a young woman named Grace and a dear old friend who is also a therapist with an interest in the mystical. Grace is interviewing him for her postgraduate studies. The therapist is a character who went through significant transformation from bad and traumatized to good and aware—he's a therapist with an interesting background.

The chapters progressively describe the linkage from wisdom of the ancients to the presence of the mystical in modern therapy. It is my intention to guide the reader on a rich journey that highlights what mysticism is and what it can be.

Probing conversations with distinguished professors of Christian theology and modern psychology shed light on the similarities between their varied cultural and professional backgrounds and their approaches to the mystical.

The final chapter, Closing the Circle, deliberates on the possible consequences of unleashing a new mystical awareness into our everyday lives by bridging our known reality and the renewed connection with the divine to attain personal fulfillment.

Let's jump right in! As you read the stories you might hear echoes of your own life experiences. Be open to seeing through a new prism and you may rediscover how wonderfully mystical your own life really is, because you are a Modern Mystic.

CHAPTER 1

Grace Is Back

"Over here!" Grace called. She was waving madly; we had not seen each other since I left the university to pursue my new career in psychotherapy. As I made my way into the airport terminal, I pondered the fact that it had been five long years. Now we were together again.

"So lovely to see you again, Grace. You look fabulous." I'm sure my eyes couldn't hide my excitement.

"You haven't changed a bit—even your hugs are the same as I remember," she said as we shared a bear hug.

"Do you have any luggage to pick up?"

"Yes, just one piece. Let's go get it," I answered as we headed toward the luggage carousel.

"How was your flight?"

"It was quite pleasant. These days I write while traveling, so the time goes fast."

"I hear there is a lot of talk about mysticism in therapy. Who would have thought it would catch on like this?" I said.

"Yes, it's a mystical phenomenon in itself," Grace said, not trying to mask her amusement. "You've aroused curiosity among a lot of people. When is your first public engagement?"

"It's starts on Wednesday, so I have a couple of days to spend with you," I answered happily.

"Wonderful!" she exclaimed. "Let's get my car quick so we don't get stuck in the afternoon traffic."

I collected my suitcase and we headed outside.

Grace lived only fifteen minutes from the airport. She was now living alone—she and her children, that is—after leaving her husband two years prior. She said she was happier now, although the loneliness is sometimes overwhelming. She said she missed me, and I certainly missed her. We had been inseparable friends ever since we first met at the university. I worked as a psychotherapy lecturer and Grace was a secretary in the university admin office. We clicked from the very beginning. Despite many differences in almost everything we knew about the world, we became fast friends.

Stuck in a difficult marriage, Grace never lost her optimism and passion for life. We refueled each other's mojo with the mutual affinity of our platonic friendship. I recalled a time when Grace tried to break off our friendship for no apparent reason other than to arrest a deepening affection that had no future. She told me that she wanted to stop hurting, and she knew I wouldn't want to let her go. At that time, I couldn't imagine life without her presence. I decided to leave Oz and move to America, partially to make it easier on both of us.

"Let me show you your room." Grace led me to the end of the house to the guest room she had prepared for me.

"You've done well, Grace," I said, looking around the room. "It must have been hard to start over on your own. I never had any doubts about you—you are an amazing woman."

"Can we start tomorrow?" Grace enquired, deftly changing the subject. "I want to complete my dissertation in the next three months. Your timing is perfect, by the way. You haven't changed; you were always there when I needed you."

"I hope we have enough time to conduct a thorough interview," Grace offered cautiously. "I've got a long list of questions to ask, if you don't mind. You and I know when we start talking it never ends," she teased.

"Yes, absolutely true! Some things never change," I laughed.

"I'll fix your favorite drink while you unpack. If you would like to take a shower, you're welcome," she called out over her shoulder as she was leaving the room.

I was thinking how happy I was to see her again. She was beautiful as ever. Why did I ever leave her? Then I remembered that there wasn't any other sensible option but to put some distance between us. Our friendship was becoming something more, drifting toward a romantic involvement. My career would have never taken off in this sleepy little town and she would never have been free to make her own choices. As much as it hurt, it was the only thing to do to preserve our beautiful friendship.

"Here's your favorite," Grace said as she handed me a cup of green tea.

"Oh thanks, Grace—you know I love it."

"Before we start tomorrow, I have a question related to the two decades before you became a psychotherapist. Is that when you worked as a photographer?" she asked.

"Yes, photography was my first professional passion. It helped me to reach out to people through the viewfinder of my camera."

"What kind of photography were you involved in?" she probed.

"I've done many types of photography, although taking people's portraits was the domain that I loved. I was pretty good at it, too.

"It might seem like an odd career shift—from photography to psychotherapy—but it really wasn't."

"How difficult was the switch?"

"It was very jarring. The way I see it now, Grace, photography was my 'initiation' into my therapy work. The process took twenty years of working in photography in Australia and America with much success. I was convinced that being a professional photographer was my life purpose, but the universe had a different plan for me. Those wonderful years in photography were just the beginning.

"I started my photography journey taking shots of couples dining in restaurants. Then I went into commercial and wedding photography. I didn't like weddings too much; it was a high-pressure job and there was loads of competition. I had a lot of fun working as an official photographer for the sponsors of the America's Cup race that was hosted for the first time outside the US after Australia won the cup. I learned the portrait trade during my three-year stint in America. When I landed back in Oz, I opened my own chain of family portrait studios.

"I called the business 'Zoom Portraits' and it was an amazing success," I continued. "Our success was due to our speedy turnaround; where the average studio would do fifty to a hundred sittings per year, Zoom was shooting between a hundred and fifty to two hundred sittings in one weekend! On top of that, Zoom delivered custom-made professional studio portraits in an hour. It doesn't sound like much of an achievement today, but this was in the days before digital photography."

"Sounds like it was a busy enterprise," Grace interjected.

"Within a short time, Zoom Portraits was the biggest purchaser of the Kodak products in the state—we were kings!" I grinned with pride.

"So what made you change course?" asked Grace.

"Well, my dream came to an abrupt halt overnight. All of a sudden there were new advisers on the scene. One in particular led my business and me right down into the void of liquidation. It broke my heart. I lost my home, all my savings, and my children's college fund, and I was in substantial debt. All I had left was my family—my wife and my two beautiful children stood by me. They literally saved my life."

"Ouch! Sudden death ..." Grace said sadly.

"Yes, but nothing happens by accident—there are causes and purposes. Sometimes we think that whatever we see with our eyes is the only reality. Although my studio was very real to me, I didn't realize at the time it was only a vehicle to propel me into something new; it led me to a new career in psychotherapy."

"How do you see the connection?" puzzled Grace.

"Let me explain: When I worked behind my camera looking through the view viewfinder, I could see a person or a group of people that were anxious and filled with anticipation. At first they were uptight and locked behind their protective shields—hiding their souls, so to speak. My task was to make them relax and find that intimate unguarded moment when they were distracted for a fraction of the second. This enabled me to penetrate their defenses, to find the crack in their protective shield. Because the camera's shutter speed allows only fraction of a second to register the image, I had to be infinitely vigilant for these cracks and extremely quick to seize the moment. My goal was always to photograph the subject's inner invisible self, rather than their physical shell—anybody can do that. But to photograph the real person, the photographer must search for and connect with his subject's soul."

"Sounds beautiful, almost mystical," Grace observed.

"Yes, the experience of connecting with people through my

camera was always extraordinary to me.

"In the therapy room, something similar occurs. The difference is that the photographer has only a fraction of a second to make the connection while the therapist has the full length of the session. In both cases, the goal is the same: to find and penetrate the cracks in the client's external, protective shell. The photographer needs to be extraordinarily vigilant as he hovers around his subject waiting for that magical moment. This is exactly how it happens during therapy. The connection shines a light on their soul, making them visible and revealing their true nature."

"I never thought of it like that," Grace said thoughtfully. "I love photographing people and I also love therapy, but I'd never made the connection between the two," she added.

"Yes, I call it 'seeing with your soul.' Our eyesight is amazing, but it's not enough to really see.

Realizing I had dominated the conversation, I took a breath and said, "I'll tell you more as we go along."

"I really look forward to it."

CHAPTER 2

A New Way of Pursuing Happiness: Epigenetics, Heart Unity, and Mysticism

How does one have a happy life?

This is the question I hear most often. In fact, my entire psychotherapy practice is based on this universal puzzle. Typically, all my clients want the same elusive thing. They don't ask directly—the question is veiled in many forms through the stories they tell. Whether it manifests itself in the sorrow of their marriage breakup, the bereavement experienced after losing a loved one, or in the challenge of living with drug addiction or depression, the fundamental question remains the same: "I am so unhappy, doc. What's wrong with me? Show me the way out of this so I can be happy again."

The answer might be complex, but these varied paths flow from the same origin.

What these individuals are really looking for is the sense of *meaning*. Happiness is not possible without meaning. Even Aristotle suggested that to attain happiness, one has to find the way to it by leading a virtuous life, a life of purpose. This explains why people who attain a vast sum of money are still unfulfilled and dissatisfied with their life. After sating their material appetites with new cars, houses, clothing, and the like—things that have no lasting meaning—they quickly lose interest and that buzz they once felt. They become unhappy. This is why so many people in affluent societies are miserable and unhappy despite having all the luxuries. Conversely, the tiny Kingdom of Bhutan is the only nation on earth that measures Gross National Happiness; this is a means of determining the quality of life, rather than the quantity of wealth. People in the more affluent countries of the first world often seek happiness by medicating their unhappiness through overeating, drugs, television, and random meaningless relationships. They lack long-lasting purpose. Their progress and growth becomes arrested often resulting in boredom and dissatisfaction. Why is this so? It's a mystery. Can it be resolved? The answer is: Of course! How? As Socrates suggested long ago, "Life without reflection is not worth living." Let's examine some of the contributing factors to this dilemma.

The environment

Environment is the key; it is one of the most important factors in shaping our lives. Think of the old saying that cautions that you will become one of those with whom you spend the most time. The environment will change you, shape you, and make you think and behave alike. A child born to an affluent family will have a totally different upbringing and better chances for greater opportunities to achieve a happy existence than a child born in the middle of a war zone, exposed to the horrors, violence, and depravation.

We humans are equipped with enormous potential. In fact,

our brains have a greater capacity for producing creative thoughts than there are hydrogen atoms in the known universe. Our bodies are amazing, ever-changing, living universes interacting with and being influenced mainly by the environment.

Sophisticated studies of physics and biology have yielded tremendous progress in expanding our understanding of the physical world. The classic model of cause and effect has been taken to task by discoveries in quantum physics that prove beyond any shadow of a doubt that the material world is generated by interactions of consciousness that transform wave-like behavior into particles of matter. This is accomplished by our brains accessing information derived from the surrounding frequency domain or field of energy comprising universal consciousness and translating this frequency into a projection we call our "reality."

An emerging area of scientific research dubbed the "New Biology" questions the conventional dogma that we are the product of our genes, and that they predetermine our destiny. If this myth were true, we would be little more than robots, dependent on the mercy of our caregivers—such as drug companies that produce chemical compounds to "regulate" our genetic deficiencies. Luckily, and right on time, the science of epigenetics comes to the rescue of common folk like you and me. Epigenetics is a branch of science that confirms that our genes *do not* predetermine a person's destiny; rather, an environment dictates the outcome. Epigenetics translates to "above the genes" ("epi" means "above," as in "epidermis"—the top layer of skin). The science of epigenetics explains that the outer membrane of each cell containing genetic material influences the gene that resides within. The cell membrane is the first point of contact with an environment, and therefore the membrane receives signals that warn cells about the impending arrival of nutrients or toxins and dictates how the cell will react.

Formerly, it was postulated that the "brain" of the cell is located inside. If the cell was driven by the nucleus (the brain of the cell at the center of the gene—as conventional biology was teaching before), then by removing the brain, the cell would die (no brain, no life). However, scientists discovered that the gene's cell lives and thrives even if this nucleus/brain is removed. This led researchers to conclude that the brain of the cell must be elsewhere. They discovered that the brain that causes the cell to function and thrive is not in the center, but on the outside of the gene cell—it's a membrane. In addition, the proteins inside the gene cell that are being influenced by the membrane are constantly moving and changing depending on the signals received from the membrane.

This astonishing discovery has enormous implications about our view of the human person. We are no longer at the mercy of predetermination based on genes passed down from generations that went before. Dr. Bruce Lipton stem cells biologist and world authority on epigenetics following his extensive studies claims that we can control our genes through mental training. We now know that our attitude toward our bodies interacts with the environment—our destiny is therefore in our own hands! Our diet, exercise routine, the quality of our thoughts (depressive or happy), emotions (love, anger, compassion), and our perception of and views on life all determine our ability to experience happiness. Most of my clients really like this idea, as it gives them the power to move from being victims back to being self-made, fate-shaping gods. You, too, can learn to take charge of your happiness.

Heart unity

In my psychotherapy practice, I use many psychological modalities aimed at assisting clients in discovering (or rediscovering) their natural potential. This ranges from a Person Centered Approach (Rogerian) which promotes the pursuit of self-actualization through Solution Focused Therapy (emphasizing a person's inner and proven strengths) to heart cohesion techniques and hypnotherapy. Heart unity or cohesion is an approach that teaches the person to focus on heart-based living; this method promotes living in compassion and developing a sense of tranquility and harmony through experiencing life in the present moment. The so called "energy medicine" has been championed by HeartMath Institute during their continuous research.

Through heart cohesion, you can learn to focus on your heart, the organ that regulates the whole body system. This exercise, which is conducted under the supervision of a therapist, is monitored on a computer screen that shows graphic heart variables for the therapist and client to view. The client is connected to the computer by a single tiny wire. The exercise is based on the empowerment of the heart, which is acting as the conductor coordinating the orchestra of the entire human system. The process typically only takes a few minutes and teaches the client to bring the heart into high cohesion, which is revealed by a green bar on the screen that rises as the client goes into deeper awareness of the heart. The results are immediate; the moment the heart takes over, the whole body relaxes as if dancing together in unity. This exercise can be immediately duplicated and practiced outside the therapy session. It is amazing to see how quickly clients learn to allow their hearts to calm down and take charge of the whole system as nature intended.

Studies have shown that the power of the heart influences the brain by sending five thousand more messages to the brain daily than the other way around. It is worth remembering that the heart is self-initiating. The heart starts the first heartbeat in week four of the embryonic development—at a time when the brain is still at the stage of forming the hollow neural tube.

What's also fascinating is that in addition to its other functions, the heart has a neurological network of forty thousand neurons (similar to those found in the brain). These connections can sense, smell, feel, and remember, just as the brain can. The heart regulates the brain that is executing all functions of the body system. The heart's memory is similar to that of the brain, except that the brain carries *images* while the heart carries *emotions* of the same event. For example, the experience of love, compassion, or a special connection is remembered in the brain as pleasant experiences, while the heart triggers the emotions that transport the person into the very feeling that was once lived. You can close your eyes now and conjure up a moment of profound love you've experienced in the past; focus on the heart space and bring the event to the heart and you will feel the event as if it were happening right now.

The mysterious way of knowing has been acknowledged since the beginning of recorded time, when the sages, poets, and artists held the heart in highest importance. They knew the power of the heart that can love or be broken. Today, many of my clients suffer from the broken heart that is being hidden behind a veil of depression. When we say, "You will succeed if you put your heart into it," we mean you must believe with all your heart, give it all you've got, love with total abandon. Living in a state of heart cohesion is to be authentic and living in the moment, experiencing life fully as it is today while creating your own reality.

Researchers confirm that the human hearts is continuously emitting frequency waves that spread out for about a two-meter radius around the body, therefore influencing the surrounding environment with these vibrations. You might have experienced times when you walked into a roomful of people and felt good or not quite right. You might have met someone that you "clicked" with and instantly the conversation was flowing with a natural rapport. That organic connection might have been due to your hearts communicating. You can test this yourself the next time you meet somebody, just by being aware of these mechanisms.

We are talking about the power of the heart—not only its physiological power, but also its power to influence our psychological and emotional states. Our heart affects our life profoundly—probably even more than our brain. The truth is, your heart can live without the brain, but the brain cannot live without the heart.

The ancients knew about the power of the heart and viewed it as the central organ that directed all of our being:

Judaism: The term "heart" (Hebrew lebab/leb [b'bel], Greek kardia [kardiva]) occurs over a thousand times in the Bible. For example, Abraham offered his weary guests food saying, "and I will fetch a morsel of bread, and strengthen ye your hearts" (Gen. 18:5).

Christianity: "Blessed are the pure of heart, for they shall see God" (Matt. 5:8).

Islam: "The Prophet Salallaahu 'alayhi wa Sallam said about your heart: Truly in the body there is a morsel of flesh which, if it be sound, all the body is sound and which, if it be

diseased, all of it is diseased. Truly it is the heart" (Muhammad al-Bukhari, Persian Islamic scholar).

We can all chose to live happy lives. Some researchers think we've all been given a natural code in the form of unique gifts and talents. Happiness is possible. We must identify these gifts and talents and take decisive action to align them with our life purpose. The consequences of following your heart or straying away from its wisdom are the feedback. When you look around and reflect, you might realize that whatever reality you are surrounded by now is the direct result of your past decisions and priorities you set for yourself.

Whatever you focus on with emotion the energy flows in that direction. Your emotions propel you into action to fulfill your newly formulated meaning.

We all have the potential and the capacity for happiness. Throughout human history people have been searching for ways to be happy. Some have confused happiness with pleasure; some sought the greater good for the greater number, as dictated by the utilitarian philosophy approach implemented by many Western countries. Some focused on people's strengths, others on compassion and love. The ancients—like Aristotle, the great philosopher and humanist—concluded that everything has its function. For example, a cup is made to carry coffee or tea, shoes are made for walking, a chair to sit on, etc. He proposed, "The function of the human person is to be happy." After a lifetime of research, Aristotle determined that in order to be happy, a person must live a virtuous life, a life of purpose (which is to say, *meaning*). On the other hand (and more recently), when asked how to attain life's happiness, Mother Theresa explained that the road to happiness leads through many failures marked by one condition: that you must never, ever give up. She worked with the poor and destitute of Calcutta, the untouchables who were hopelessly dying despite the herculean efforts of Mother Theresa and her team. Though she suffered many failures, she never gave up her mission. She asserted that the meaning of true love is to give until it hurts.

We all want to be happy, therefore when we are not, we desperately search for ways to get back to our natural state of being: happiness.

Mysticism

This book is about us. We can describe ourselves in many ways: beings with the freewill to create of our own destiny, beings driven by intelligence and choices, beings driven by curiosity that compels us to pursue progress. We love to see ourselves growing and expressing our compassion toward others, we are playful and purposeful, and we have a deep need to connect with the divine. Our sense of awe and wonder is often expressed in our spirituality, channeled through our work that we love. Occasionally when we stop to capture the moment in time while enjoying and absorbing the mystery of life, we become Modern Mystics.

My clinical observations over many years lead me to my

understanding of the meaning of "mystical." The mystical event or life is a personal experience during which the person feels special connection to the greatest power of Wisdom and Truth. The event can resemble a religious experience, however, any person of any cultural or philosophical background can experience it. As a professional observer of human behavior, I have observed certain patterns of behavior that allow people to connect with the mystical. From asylum seekers who escaped torture and war, to people traumatized by divorce or the death of a loved one, to those who have fought to overcome drug addiction—they all have one thing in common: the resolve to overcome adversaries and to return to happiness. I've found that humans possess remarkable courage and the will to succeed. There is no doubt that we all share something mystical about us.

Many people experience the mystical without even being aware of it. One primary characteristic of a mystical experience is an extraordinary sense of calm; others might include:

- A sense of unity or totality with the universe or the divine
- A sense of timelessness (time distortion)
- A sense of having encountered ultimate reality (something real, not just a projection or hallucination)
- Spontaneous amazement (experiencing the unknown for the first time)
- A sense of sacredness (humbling surrender of ego)
- A sense that one cannot adequately describe the richness of this experience (phenomenon like no other)
- Mystical experiences may last only a few seconds or they may produce a lingering buzz that lasts up to several days. The mystical experience may resemble a hypnotic trance

characterized by time distortion and dissociation, though the person is not under hypnosis in the conventional sense. A mystical experience can be an awareness that morphs natural reality and illusion—for example, the greenness of grass, the songs of birds, the sound of leaves rustling in the trees, and the connection between people in love and their individual perception. As in a "lucid dream," we know that we are dreaming and we are therefore able to influence our dream.

Mysticism is neither a faith, nor a belief; neither is it a principle or a dogma.

A mystic is born a person, like each of us, who is exposed to truth and understanding. We all naturally pursue a conscious or subconscious search for meaning, but the mystical experience reaches beyond conventional rational understanding or knowing.

Being a mystic involves having a certain temperament, a certain outlook on life, a certain insight. Some people are confused by the word "mystic"—that's understandable, as mysticism cannot be fully explained in plain words. It must be experienced.

A mystic can be any person who studies life. Through our work, family commitments, relationships, successes, failures, perseverance, and emotions (love, anger, compassion, sadness), we are all mystics. Being a Modern Mystic means to pursue and connect with the ultimate source of happiness.

Mysticism occurs while embracing the connection that is expressed in the most subtle manifestations of a person's insight firsthand. It can be a result of direct connection with the Ultimate

Power or human interaction on a deep, soulful level. Once the exchange of such energy starts to flow, the parties involved forge a profound collaboration, gravitating in this union toward an ultimate desire of every human heart: to tap the Divine Spirit of Happiness.

Science of mysticism

But what of the gulf between spirituality and science? As the mystical cannot be reproduced in a laboratory, it has been rejected as unscientific or downright absurd. With the help of recent discoveries of the New Physics, which is based on a better understanding of quantum physics, many physicists postulate that the resurrection can be scientifically explained. Following observations of the subatomic environments, scientists concluded that something unexplained and mystical is occurring on the physical plane. The protons and electrons seem to randomly interact without apparent contact and what is really making things move is what is occurring in the space between and around them. Particles within atoms are just like planets: they are not physically connected and that very lack of connectivity makes everything about how they work so mysterious. As all things in our physical universe must follow the same laws (although this formula may still not be known to us at this point), it seems that our entire world is similarly unconnected. It would appear that "empty" spaces filled with energy between the atoms, quarks, or planets can make things "mysteriously" work.

Some of the recent discoveries establish connections between the reality of the world as we know it (or perceive it) and what is actually real. In the seventeenth century, Descartes observed that what we see is not what is actually happening; yet that is only the first step toward a new consciousness. The resurrection of Jesus Christ remains the greatest mystery known to man. The resurrection can be philosophically explained—even successfully defended by our common law that would decree that the resurrection has taken place beyond any reasonable doubt. However, this is not enough for science. Many theoreticians offered a variety of propositions on the subject, however, as it is driven by reason (backed by empirical evidence), science was unwilling to dismiss the Standard Model of physics. The so-called "New Physics" suggests that quantum physics offers a plausible scientific explanation for the resurrection.

John von Neumann, a prominent mathematician and physicist, believed that "consciousness is a living entity that is made up of some real things (energy flow) between solid particles." For him, materialism lost its importance in favor of something mysterious and probably unimaginable. Moreover, modern physicists propose ideas far removed from the classical materialism paradigm. In his book, *Advanced Quantum Mechanics*, the iconoclastic physicist Freeman Dyson hypothesized that human thoughts and feelings might one day be downloaded into magnetic fields composed of clouds of photons and gravitons, long after galaxies and stars have ceased to exist, if the universe continues to expand as it is now. Also, in his Omega Point theory, Frank Tipler proposed that such intelligences would be able to replicate or resurrect all conscious beings that have ever existed, so that we might find ourselves replicated billions of years in the future. And Lee Smolin argued that future intelligent beings might be able to download themselves through wormholes in space–time into other parallel universes, so that a sort of immortality would be possible.

Although some may conclude that such propositions sound like science fiction, the fact that they come from reputable and strictly scientific communities is encouraging in a field where the mystery of life after death was considered as fantasy. Our willingness to at least consider the possibilities is growing; are we not accustomed to the idea that the virtual reality of a computer download can be as real to any human (especially the "digitally native" young) as our "analog" reality?

The reality of the behavior of particles on the subatomic level can help us to imagine the unimaginable—that something can occur out of "nothing" or mysteriously seem to vanish and reappear. Our skepticism is the result of our learned perception rather than true reality.

Consider the following example: Let's say we were living in the perfectly flat world with no concept of three-dimensional space. We could not look up into space, and even if we did, we would not be able to "see" anything for in our consciousness space would not exist at all. Therefore, any visitations from "above" would not be felt or "seen" until it appeared (seemingly miraculously) from "nowhere." Interestingly, it would disappear into thin air as quickly as it had revealed itself to us just the same!

Mysticism in music

The characteristics of mystical experience have strong relevancy to musical experience. Musicologist Julius Portnoy believed that musical experience is in fact a mystical experience. According to

Portnoy, "The mystical qualities in music are greater than in any other art." He suggests that mysticism in music is related to:

1. The state of the listener who is in the present moment while cooperating between psychological and emotional areas of being that are derived from the listener's beliefs. Portnoy states that music without mysticism is like religion without mysteries. He further compares holy images to how we respond to musical tones.
2. Human curiosity that leads the composer to explore music in the context of personal awe and wonder. He says that without human curiosity, the composer would not be able to tap into spiritual awakening.
3. Oneness. The composer or listener must submerge themself into and become one with music. Music then transports them into the mystical realm of another world. By becoming one through music, we form a relationship with the universe, and we may then discover ourselves from a different point of view.

Mystical sounds that unify us through, for example, the godly music of Bach, can be viewed as an emotional cry for connection with the supernatural as expressed in blues music or the mysterious impact of Mozart's compositions. We are persistently reminded that the mysterious is present all around us, if only we are prepared to tune in and listen.

CHAPTER 3

New Physics: Mystical links between Science and New Reality

What constitutes the mystical? Is it just a concept revolving around the special connection between religious seekers and their God? New science is helping explain the mystical through quantum physics and the nature of perceptions. Are we Modern Mystics, then, if we indulge our curiosity in the mysterious by tapping into the unknown through ancient writings linked with fresh theories in science?

I love Michael Talbot. He was an amazing visionary on the subject of the holographic universe. Unfortunately he passed away few years ago, however his legacy remains and grows in popularity. He talked about the phenomenon of perception: everything that surrounds us is subject to our perception. Therefore, since everything is *conceived* and *perceived* by our minds, there is nothing actually "out there." No colors, no smells, no sounds—nothing. Yet it is very real to us. Talbot (and now a whole raft of scientists) believes this perception is created by the holographic universe in which we are immersed (as opposed to looking at the hologram from outside-in). Being inside the hologram makes it extremely difficult to determine what kind of reality we are surrounded by—is it a real world that surrounds us or an elusive perception created by the hologram that we are immersed in? Some of the scientific researchers suggest that we are living in a hologram, and nothing is real except our perceptions. The brain is not a source of thoughts, only a receiver of the holographic information that exists outside our brain.

> *"Your brain first receives the hologram in waves frequency downloaded from the Field. It then translates those waves into particles to create your holographic 'physical reality,' and then sends that 'reality' 'out there' for you to perceive and experience." Prof. John-Dylan Haynes*

The scientific researchers confirm that our brains know what is going to happen before we decide. Experiments were conducted to identify the source of our decisions; for example, the decision to react in a certain way after being exposed to either happy or sad, calm or traumatic images. The subject watched a monitor where images were projected, and subject's task was to react accordingly. Another computer was observing the subject's brain function. The computer could predict ahead of time what emotional decision the subject would make. The conscious decision could be predicted up to six seconds before the subject registered a conscious decision.

In another study, a computer observing a spot inside the brain that indicates whether the subject is going to press the right button or the left button with 100 percent accuracy. This means that there is some sort of unconscious activity that the brain is tapping, as if something outside the brain supplies a mechanism that tells the brain how to react.

This can only be explained by the idea that the brain is a receiver of information that comes from the field of frequencies in which we are all immersed. This is consistent with the double-slit experiment, proving that waves collapse into matter when they are being observed or focused on by some conscious being—for example, a human or God.

We know we are real when it comes to emotions. Emotions somehow fall outside of the mind, our psyche, or even our perception. Emotions seem to stand alone. It seems that emotion is the cardinal element of our being. Everything else is either a judgment or perception based on the former conditioning that we've been subjected to.

Perception plays a huge role in the human psyche

There is a TV series called "Dexter" in which the main character is a serial killer. He solves crimes but also goes after the guilty. If for some reason they cannot be brought to justice, he kills them based on his own judgment. The viewer perceives him to be a hero, despite knowing that he is a serial killer. The viewer therefore condones the act of killing. Most people condemn killing as being wrong, but sometimes the same act can be justifiable. There are many examples on both sides of the issue: state-sponsored murder by the Nazis, ethnic cleansing in the former Yugoslavia, capital punishment, or deaths that occur in war.

It is not *what* we look at, but *how* we look that matters. We make our own reality. Quantum physics is an excellent reminder of this. The subatomic particles behave differently when they are being observed and when no one is watching. We are all made up of these particles and when they are being observed, you can see their "obedient" behavior, in keeping with the classical laws of physics. However, they turn into waves when the observer is not looking. This is the basis for the saying, "You can judge the person by what they do when no one else is watching." But how can you tell? Only the person involved knows—no one else. So it is impossible to really know what someone else is up to. If you knew exactly what a person was doing or thinking, would you know their true nature?

The Schrödinger's cat experiment tells us that we can never be certain.

In 1935 Edwin Schrödinger proposed an experiment to explain "superposition" on the subatomic level where two particles can be simultaneously present in two different states (please note: it's only a philosophical thought experiment—no cats were used or harmed in any way!).

A cat is put in a sealed box for an hour. A radioactive material is placed in the box as well. If only one atom of the radioactive material decays inside the box, it sends a signal to a decay detector placed in the box and a hammer falls, killing the cat. There is fifty-fifty chance the cat is dead or alive inside of the box. No one would ever know the outcome until the box is opened; only the act of looking inside can determine the truth. If no one is looking inside the box, the reality is two faced, uncertain. Since we don't know the outcome, the cat could either be dead or alive—the cat exists in a dual state simultaneously! Is the observer causing the cat to be dead or alive? And are the two possibilities happening simultaneously?

This question has profound consequences on the perceived reality of the universe. If the observer is causing reality just by observing the cat then who is observing the observer? There must be something or someone of greater capability to do this—another consciousness perhaps? Maybe it's the field in which we are all immersed? Maybe God, as architect-creator, is moving all things in an intelligent manner? Or are we living in multiple universes simultaneously; meaning that everything is happening at the same time. For example, we are living in the twenty-first century reality, and at the same time we are living in the ancient world—say, alongside dinosaurs, plus all the other possibilities clustered together into a single moment.

But how can this be? The holographic universe theory sheds some light on this paradox. If everything is just a projection and not really real, then there is no conflict with any number of universes existing simultaneously. Because they are not real, they cannot interfere with one another. A hologram is not real, even though it looks real. It's like watching the news on TV. We know that the people inside the TV are not in our living room, nor are they inside the TV set. The news anchor is sitting in a studio in some distant location; it's only an *image* that is projected, not the physical self.

Still, whoever is operating the studio that is transmitting this image to your TV set temporarily exerts control over your mind. Your mind is reacting to the images by employing your own senses. When you switch off the TV set, and the images disappear, your reality shifts and the TV set becomes just another piece of static furniture. So in this view of reality, we experience no actual sound, no images, no smells, no taste, no touch. It's all in our heads—it's all illusion—as in a dream.

The perception of reality is completely dependent on the perceiver. The sensitivity of sight or touch is individually determined and is subject to continuous change. It can be enhanced or it can deteriorate.

Selective perception

A couple I counseled who had been married for thirty years reported that over the years their physical intimacy gradually waned. Not because they loved each other any less. No. Rather, after years of physical contact, they had become somewhat desensitized. The husband reported that his wife had become less interested in his body. And for his part, he admitted that her body didn't turn him on the same as it had during their courtship. The man started to think that he was not able to satisfy his wife and that his sex drive was diminishing. Medical professionals he consulted told him his testosterone level had lowered, so he feels less sexual arousal. He accepted that diagnosis. He asked his doctor about Viagra. With the help of the "little blue pill," he gained renewed confidence and felt like a brand new man. For a little while, he was satisfied and so was his wife. But after a while, the Viagra didn't seem to work as well. So he increased the dose. His sex drive continued to wane. Disenchanted and concerned about his racing heart, he gave up on the Viagra and decided he was just getting too old for sex.

Unfortunately, despite their long-term marriage, the couple soon divorced. As it turned out, sex was not the only complaint that made this couple unhappy. They had been gradually drifting apart for some time. After a period of grieving following their separation, the man realized that his interest in women had not diminished. On the contrary, he found himself noticing them even more often than before—the "forbidden fruit" that he would never have the chance of picking ever again. One fateful day he met a woman twenty years his junior. He treated her like his daughter at first, but then she began to show signs of interest in him that were definitely *not* paternal. He was confused, but flattered, so he decided to enjoy the ride. He didn't know why he turned her on—was it his charm, his maturity that she found so appealing? She perceived his charm to be romantic advances, so she responded. Soon they become lovers. At first he was rusty—he was out of practice—however, he became the stallion he once was. Egged on by this energetic young woman, he is having wild sexual encounters more frequently and passionately than ever before—even when he was in his twenties! What happened?

His problem was not the result of low testosterone levels, it was a matter of desire—it had everything to do with his *perception*. When his senses focused on the "new prize," his physiology responded. He found new meaning in life, the meaning that says, "maybe I am older, but with the right tools (of encouragement) I can feel brand new again!" His perception of this newly created reality changed in keeping with his renewed self-confidence.

Ordinary experience and quantum physics

Quantum physics explains this phenomenon by proving that the object observed and focused on changes its behavior. For example the now famous double-slit experiment proves beyond any doubt that matter is influenced by something other than just "cause and effect," that classical model of physics asserted by Newton. Quantum physics proves that by mere conscious observation (focusing), the observed matter changes. Here's how it works:

A researcher installs a gun that shoots subatomic particles onto a screen. Between the screen and the gun another screen is installed, but this one has a slit to allow the particles to pass through. The experiment is designed to register the pattern formed on the screen on the other side of the screen with the slit.

The gun fires, the particles travel through the slit in the first screen and predictably form a pattern on the on the screen behind.

The researcher then replaces the screen with the slit with one that has two slits for the particles to pass through. It is expected that the particles will travel either through one slit or the other and form the pattern on the receiving screen accordingly. But the particles traveling through two slits form a pattern of waves of energy rather than two identical patterns from each slot. What happened? How did the particles become waves of energy when they were clearly particles of matter? How can the particles be matter and the energy at the same time?

The scientist decided to peek, and in the third stage of the experiment they placed monitors to watch what was going on. Which of these slots are the particles traveling through? Are they interfering with each other, and if so, in what way?

Now something mystical happened. Just by being observed, the particles returned to their original state and behaved as particles, not as waves. They now formed a pattern of individual holes on the receiving screen. Simply put: the unobserved particles changed into waves of energy just by being observed or focused upon.

This discovery has profound consequences for our understanding of life and the rules that govern our universe. It applies to the whole universe equally, including our relationships here on Earth. It indicates that when we focus on something (matter) the object that we are monitoring changes its behavior from its "natural," original state into something new and tangible. When we don't focus (or monitor), the particles are subject to the field that they are immersed in and therefore behave like waves, unformulated and shapeless, ready to be formed into meaning.

In our world

We are immersed in the field of frequencies until our brain translates them into meaning. There is no escape, just as there is no escape for a fish born and swimming in the ocean (unless fish is caught and taken out of the water—but this is another possibility that we may discuss elsewhere). The fish is part of the ocean. It reacts to the ocean currents and other vibrations caused by the ecology of the oceanic system. This is the same for us; we are living in the "ocean of the energy field"—we are immersed in it. This we cannot escape; we are all born into this reality. In our mother's womb, we "think" that this is our native environment, so we get cozy and comfortable until our birth time, when we are expelled from the womb and into the vast new reality of the "energy ocean." Suddenly we are literally blinded by this new reality—the bright light, the many sounds, the sensation of cold, the foreign smells, the bad taste in our mouth, the excruciating pain as our delicate body stretches on its way through the birth canal. The entire body from the top of our head to the bottom of our toenails aches as it is stretched to its limits.

This is the first trauma that we all experience. Welcome to the new world of energy! At birth, our brand new senses can't make any sense of what's going on, it's complete chaos. The only communication we manage to initiate with the new world is the sound that is perceived as crying. It is not really crying—this is the primal scream expressing the happiness of arrival. It's just like when we arrive in a new place when traveling: although we may be exhausted from the trauma of our journey, we are always happy and curious about being in the new place. We may not scream when checking into our hotel, we may jump on the bed with childlike joy! It's a new place, it signals new opportunities, new possibilities. At birth we are completely fresh and ready for new experiences. The surprises of the strange reality we will encounter in our new environment will come later.

Although this chaos is new, foreign, and completely unexpected, we are nevertheless curious. Soon enough we are being placed on our mother's chest. The closeness of her body feels very familiar and naturally comfortable. I can hear the sound of my mother's heart. This sound calms any of my doubts about the new world instantly. I am safe after all. My mother, my anchor is here, I have no fear. God forbid the anchor should ever disappear! It would mess up my new life, I'm sure. I thank God immediately. He knows!

My own mother had me for the first three years of my life. I didn't know if this was a long time or short. I didn't care. I loved her with all my heart. I not only believed, but I knew that my mother, my anchor would be there forever. I couldn't conceive that one day she would disappear from my life as suddenly as the blink of an eye. All of the love that I knew would be gone in an instant. Even when she died I still couldn't get it. I thought that death only kills my love, not her. I was convinced that she traveled somewhere, but without me. My dad told me that she is in heaven. I remember our conversation: "Dad, where is mum? He replied, "Mum is in heaven." I said, "I want to go there, when can I go there?" He answered, "Not yet, though one day you will." It is amazing that I still remember this conversation. According to the modern scientific assumptions a three-year-old child cannot possibly remember a conversation at that young age. Well, maybe I am an extraordinary man (like everyone else), but I do remember. When your emotions are so high and the feeling of love and longing for love is that strong, then yes, you do remember, regardless of your age.

What about trauma?

Traumatic experience is connected with the surrounding energy field more than with your conscious brain. Therefore, information based on your emotions is somehow registered inside the field and you can tap into it and relive it. This indicates that trauma doesn't really reside in the brain, but is stored in the field and is there for eternity. Your memory can fade but the field remembers, or rather stores, the information. The field is like the ocean. If a fish poops into the ocean it stays there. Of course it is diluted and transformed into something different, but it doesn't disappear. If you had a time machine, you could go back to the time when the fish was depositing his poop. This is what's happening with trauma—it never really disappears. Everyone has been traumatized; being born is the first and most obvious example that everybody has experienced. The images of trauma can haunt a person forever. Not all the time, but only when the person becomes emotionally vulnerable. The human emotions are causing the person to relive the trauma. The memories don't really live in the brain, they are stored in the field, and the way to access them is through the power of our emotions. The field of energy is like a huge computer hard drive. The brain is just the computer's processor. The emotions are the channel to our reality. Our perception of reality is fuelled by our emotions. Our reality is the product of our emotions put into action. If you're angry, you may channel this emotion into action. On the other hand, if the emotion you're experiencing is love and compassion, the opposite action will be created. Therefore, our emotions must be pure and useful. There is no point in addressing hate with hate; it is ineffective, destructive, and uncreative, and it always leads to a dead end.

Our brain decodes the frequency that comes from the field in which we are immersed. Like a computer that decodes binary codes comprising zeros and ones and converts them into letters, words, and images we can comprehend, our brain receives seemingly chaotic and meaningless frequencies of information from the energy field that surrounds us and translates them into coherent information. The information is passed on from the holographic universe that is an illusion in itself—a mirage, a phantom. So our brains are trying to make sense of an illusion. As this information enters an individual brain, that brain is creating the new hologram. If the hologram were universal, we would all have this same identical perception about things. For example, if someone exclaims, "Hey, that guy looks like President Obama!" you may not see the resemblance at all. You are seeing the same person, however your perception is entirely different. Another good example is how people who witnessed the same road accident often have completely different perceptions of what happened.

Adjust your focus

Sometimes people try too hard. They often think about concepts by over-analyzing them and then they get discouraged. I sometimes tease a friend by saying that I have a sixth sense—I can see a person not with my eyes, but by intuition. In fact, we all do it. "How?" she asks. "Well," I say, "how many times have you seen somebody acting like a child? You can see there is an adult standing in front of you, yet you are convinced that what you are 'seeing' is a child. How does it happen? Do you really see a child? Yes, but how do you see it? Is it through your eyes or through your other senses?" I had this conversation with a friend who recited a passage from the New Testament in which Christ related the parable about the people who have eyes but do not see. What does it mean? Is it possible to "see" beyond our sense of sight? The answer is, of course! We are all capable of doing it and we have done it many times, but we discount the existence of a sixth sense.

People who claim they see auras are talking about colorful halos around people's bodies. So, they would seem to be relying on the sense of sight. Great! My question would be: As our sense of sight deteriorates with age, would the ability to see auras also diminish? The same would presumably apply to those who claim to be able to hear certain unusual frequencies. How disappointing! However, if we distance ourselves from the deceptive nature of our five senses for a moment and move closer to our intuition (or tapping into the energy field), we may discover something truly remarkable. If we focus on the energy (which we all possess and can exchange) rather than the conventional senses, we can "see" a lot more. We can see adults acting like children, people shape-shifting into something other than what they really are, and so on. For example: "He's a wolf in the sheep's clothing." How do we know this? By focusing on the energy field, we are creating something new, we are beginning to see beyond our senses—just as the quantum physics experiment in which the object that we pay attention to changes its behavior, from wave into particle of matter.

These discoveries have profound consequences on our relationships. In my psychotherapy practice, I often encounter couples displaying a lack of communication because their focus is elsewhere. If one person is consumed by his or her career or other outside relationship, the other person suffers from being invisible; they perceive themselves as being ignored and unacknowledged. This leads to disagreements, arguments, or seeking satisfaction elsewhere. The human need unmet will find the way to satisfaction. If the "hungry" person is invited to the banquet full of delicious delicacies, it's only a matter of time before they will dive in. If one person needs diversity and the other more stability, and the two parties don't focus on each other to recognize the pattern of dissatisfaction, the relationship is destined to gradually disintegrate. We only exist if we are the object of meaningful focus. In fact nothing exists without conscious focusing. Simply close your eyes and the world disappears. It is because when your shift your focus, the world of your own perception follows.

CHAPTER 4

My Mother's Eyes:
An Encounter with the Mystical

"Tell me more about yourself," Grace prompted.

"What would you like to know?" I queried.

"Tell me about your mother."

"Why?"

"Because you talk about her quite often."

"Do I?"

"Yes," she responded with thinly veiled impatience.

"I didn't really know her, although I think about her every single day. It's been so long ago. I have very few memories of her. I don't even remember her beautiful face."

"How do you know she was beautiful then?" Grace goaded.

"I know her instinctively, besides I have a couple of photos to confirm it—one of my parents' wedding, and one taken in the middle of the crop field when she was a teenager. I don't remember my mother's face, still I *know* her. I've always known her. If I could meet her again, I would not look for the image of her face—those photos that remind me of her— because they don't. My eyes would deceive me. I would recognize her by feeling her in my heart and by her unforgettable touch."

"What do you mean?" She prodded gently.

"You see, thanks to my mother's tenderness, I've developed a memory of her that extends beyond the five senses. She left me because she died when I had just turned three—my birthday was in January and she passed away in March. Some researchers say that the toddler's brain cannot remember images from that far back. It may be true, because I don't remember my mother's face. What I do remember is the *feeling* of her. I don't know how to explain it. People who are affected by blindness say that they can "see" by touching. The sense of touch for them is the most important. I remember meeting a blind person who wasn't blind from birth, so she was able to remember what is it was like to see with her own eyes. When I asked her which sense would she rather have— the sense of touch or the sense of sight—she responded without hesitation that the sense of touch is far superior to the sense of sight. She said if she had to make a choice between the two, she would never give up the sense of touch. She would never swap her sense of touch for anything else—including her eyesight.

"Are you talking about the concept of 'seeing' that actually doesn't involve the sense of sight?" she asked.

"Yes, precisely," I said. "It is in the realm of what is related in the scriptures: 'They have eyes, yet they cannot see.' I am also reminded of a parable about Jesus meeting the apostles after his resurrection. Are you interested?"

"Yes, of course! Do tell," Grace exclaimed with a broad smile.

"Well the story goes that Jesus, after returning from the dead, revealed himself to his friends. Of course, they recognized him instantly, though as the storyteller describes, Jesus's body was somehow transformed. On seeing him, his friends believed that he was in fact the resurrected messiah—but not all of them. One of the apostles, Thomas, was absent on that supernatural 'visitation day.' When Thomas reunited with the others, they told him that they saw Jesus alive, but Thomas refused to believe them. He saw Jesus being killed by crucifixion only three days before. So Thomas said: 'I will not believe until I see Jesus's wounds and I put my own hands in each of them.' That's how he came to be known as 'doubting Thomas.'

"According to the storyteller, Jesus visited his friends again. However, this time Thomas was present. When he saw Jesus, Thomas instantly realized that what the apostles were telling him about Jesus had in fact been true. Jesus approached Thomas and asked him to see for himself if he was the same person Thomas knew before the resurrection. Jesus invited Thomas to inspect the wounds he had sustained while hanging on the cross. Jesus encouraged Thomas to 'see,' saying, 'Put your finger here; look here are my hands. Give me your hand; put it in my side. Doubt no longer, but believe.' Thomas was embarrassed to test his master like that. Out of respect for Jesus and his own embarrassment, Thomas didn't want to put his hands into Jesus's wounds, but Jesus insisted. Thomas placed his hands into the wounds. Only then was he fully convinced. Thomas realized that here before him stood the same Jesus that died on the cross. The outcome of this meeting was Jesus's famous comment to Thomas: 'You believe because you can see me. Happy are those who have not seen, and yet believed.'"

"That's a beautiful story, even if it's just a story," Grace said softly. " I never knew the whole story, thank you."

I replied lightheartedly, "*Ha, ha!* So much wisdom in these old books. Many sayings and parables come from these and others ancient writings. So much so that sometimes we use the phrases in our everyday lives not realizing their origins. The 'doubting Thomas' story is a perfect example.

"Sometimes we look for wisdom in faraway places, when it is right under our nose. It's like another old saying: 'The darkest place is under the candlestick.'"

Grace chortled, "So true! But you were going to tell me about your mother."

"OK, something really strange happened to me recently. I went to this seminar in Gold Coast, a marvelous event. The presenter was Tony Robbins, a performance coach who helps people who want more out of this life than just the routine stuff of everyday living. He motivates people to take action—to 'seize the day!' The *New York Times* calls **Robbins** 'the **high priest** of human potential.' He's advised and coached people from all walks of life, including Bill Clinton, Oprah, Hugh Jackman, Quincy Jones, Serena Williams and many, many more. He has been called an 'über coach of whom the world can't seem to get enough.'

Tony is like no other coach. My wife and I were invited to spend six wonderful days fully immersed in his coaching world. It was stimulating for physical, mental, emotional, and spiritual learning. On the first day of the event, Tony walked on stage and greeted everyone by saying, 'You are going to get what you came here for; however, this is not what you came here for.' I am sure that these words aroused curiosity among the two thousand delegates gathered in the huge conference hall. Certainly for me, by the end of the event this statement came true," I exclaimed happily.

"I've heard of him. I haven't attended any of his events, but I've heard they are amazing. So, c'mon—what happened to you?"

"Oh yes, something quite unexpected!" I replied.

"What—did you learn how not to go to the toilet for the whole day?" she chided.

"Well Tony does it!" I laughed. "It seems to be true—the guy doesn't take breaks for anything!

"Well, what happened was this: This is still about my mother; you interested?"

"Yes, yes. That's why I'm here—I'm all ears," she said.

"Well, we were asked to participate in a form of guided meditation. I'm not big on meditation; in fact, I don't know exactly how to meditate 'properly' other than to sit in silence and just observe my breathing. Hey, the Dalai Lama promotes this simple method of observing your breathing, so I go with the expert!

"On that evening," I continued, "the mood was set. The idea was to relax the mind and observe what will emerge. I was happy to comply. I closed my eyes and followed instructions. Immersing myself in this meditation, I quickly lost a sense of time. I felt good and warm although the temperature in the room was only twenty-one degrees—heck, it was twenty-eight outside!

"The main lights were dimmed and creating an ambient atmosphere," I lowered my voice and spoke more slowly and softer now, "Tony was in charge of guiding the whole audience. It felt like a form of hypnotic trance where people were encouraged to follow instructions. I was game.

"Following a series of audio prompts and visualizations projected on a large screen, I closed my eyes and slowly drifted into a deeply relaxed state. While my eyes were shut, something strange happened: I suddenly saw an eye emerging right in front of me. It seemed to be in the middle of my head and it was as prominent as it was real. The eye was blinking and I could see all the details, such as the eyebrow and individual eyelashes clearly." I complemented this word-picture by "drawing" the image with hand gestures.

"Somehow I almost immediately recognized this eye—a living, blinking eye in the middle and on the inside of my forehead. The eye was gazing at me with peace and loving kindness. This lasted for some time and then the eye disappeared as quickly as it had appeared. I was not aware of the time. Simultaneously, as the one eye disappeared, it was replaced by a *pair* of eyes—and they were both looking at me just as that single eye before. These eyes were real!" I couldn't contain my excitement.

"They were also complete, with eyebrows and eyelashes. The eyes were blinking from time to time in slow motion and I felt very warm and deeply at peace. I thought to myself: 'I know these eyes.' I was looking at them and they were looking at me. It was a mysterious and magical moment.

"I was awakened momentarily by Tony's voice gently urging us to go back in time further still. Without hesitation and without much effort I felt that my mother was holding me in her arms. I looked at her and she looked back at me. The moment was extraordinary—total immersion in profound love and peace. I know the eyes were my mother's. I don't know her face, but I know her eyes. Now I am lying in her arms cuddled in her breast, feeling totally secure and more loved than I've ever felt before or since.

"I should add," I explained, "that my mother was diagnosed with a brain tumor, so she became increasingly unwell. She had several operations. My mum became paralyzed and was bedridden. As I said, I was only three years old. I don't remember my mother's face. I only remember her intuitively, emotionally. I don't remember her voice, nor her face, touch, smell, or taste, however I can recall all of that intuitively. I can't explain it. It's like 'seeing by intuition.' I feel that I know my mother beyond the five senses."

"That's fascinating," Grace intoned, barely able to mask her growing enthusiasm.

"Yes, it's been puzzling me and has fascinated me all my life.

"Ok, let's go back to my hypnotic session," I proposed with a smile.

"I hear the question, quite out of nowhere: 'Who else is in the room?' Tony asked. Now I immediately feel the presence of God. Divine energy envelops the scene. There is no doubt in my mind that God is in the room, hovering and making this embrace possible. The feeling of God's love is profound and unmistakable. My mother and I just look deeply into each other's eyes and nothing else matters. This was a moment of transcendent love in its purest form," I uttered, my eyes welling up with tears. I paused.

"In that divine moment, I completely understand and I realize that I am made of love. It is as if God communicated directly with me, in these words:

'The love is everlasting, you are made of me, your mother is made of me, and so is everyone else! The love is the only real and beautiful thing. Do not ever be afraid to love you must spread your love everywhere. The years of fear and resentment, pain, and sorrow are over. This is what I want you to know: YOU ARE LOVE, YOU ARE SAFE, YOU ARE HERE, YOU ARE NEVER ALONE.'"

I had to stop for a moment to regain my composure.

"Now, I felt a complete reconciliation with God. It was my return to God after years of resentment. Only now I felt at peace." I became emotional and I teared up again, only more so.

"Wow!" Grace exclaimed. "This is such an amazing experience! Do you still meditate, and do you often get this kind of realization while meditating?" she asked.

"Oh heavens no! I have never ever experienced anything

remotely similar to this before or since," I replied with conviction. "It was true mysticism in action—oneness with my mother, oneness with the universe, oneness with God, and a complete oneness with myself.

"Now that you got me going Grace, do you really want to hear more?" I teased.

"Oh yes, you know I do!" Grace responded.

"OK, at this point I heard Tony say, 'Go back in time even more.' So now, I regress further and find myself as a baby lying on a hard surface in some sort of pain—I'm crying. Right above me there is a bright light that blinds me. Interestingly, I can describe what I see: the light is the globe inside the socket of the primitive lamp shade that looks like a metallic dish hanging down from the ceiling. No one is around, but I hear voices. I know that I'm not alone. I'm cold. Then I sense my mother is approaching. She wraps me in something warm and picks me up. I feel warm and safe instantly. My pain stops; my crying stops. My mother holds me near. I feel entirely safe now, as I am lying wrapped and cuddling into her breast. I look at her and all I can see is the most beautiful pair of eyes. Everything else around me is nonexistent. I realize that these are the same eyes I saw before, only now they have a context: these are my mother's eyes!" I blurted out with childlike exuberance.

"I am back in that moment again. My mother's eyes are the most loving and beautiful sight-feeling I have ever experienced. The feeling of profound love fills me entirely. I don't want to let go, so we stay closely together. There is no time passing at all.

Everything stops, except the feeling of the absolute love that we are both immersed in.

"She looks back at me. We are looking at each other. I feel the deepest love and compassion I've ever felt in my life. Have you ever wondered, 'What is truth?'" I looked at Grace for confirmation. "This is the moment of truth—a mother and her son, locked in an instant of complete love, surrendered to each other. I have a deep sense of realization: *we are one.*

"Grace, this is the closest I've ever come to a true mystical moment. You know, I've always been interested in mysticism. I read about it and discussed it on many occasions with some insightful people. I don't know how to explain what mysticism actually is, but I believe that this encounter should give you a pretty good idea."

"You said it so beautifully. I think I know what you mean now," Grace said.

Observations

This is a typical account of a hypnotic trance: the distortion of time and the realization of the "other place"; the change of physiological, mental, emotional, and spiritual states; the new-formed perception of reality.

Dissociation is what allows the subject to imagine being on another plane in another place, often unknown.

Recalling past events: This works on the premise that if you have experienced a deep sensation—emotional, psychological, or spiritual—you will begin to reexperience the sensation again, as if it was happening again, now, with this same intensity. Therefore, if you remember that you were happy or sad, this feeling will come back again you will be reliving it as if it was happening right now, and as intense as ever.

In this case, the meaning reemerged as he reported: "I realized that love did not die with my mother. I possessed a love that always dwelled inside of me. Love endures; it exists forever. I knew in that instant that I could now "unleash this love on the world." It's clear that this love has been suppressed for all this time, ever since I saw my mother in her coffin—my last memory of her. For me love was dead".

"However, through this meditative experience my love was resurrected. I have a reason to believe that love is alive again. The experience has been absolutely real for me. I had to "see" it to believe it". The resemblance to the "doubting Thomas" story can be helpful to illustrate the power of the mind when it focuses. We all possess these qualities, yet we rarely use them; or rather, we do not use them enough to conquer our deepest fears, fears that prevent us from returning to our natural state—*happiness*.

Homework

Let's develop a new meaning; let's change the story from "tragic to magic." The energy is attracted to whatever you focus on. When you focus, this energy will change the physiology of your body. Now you are ready to form a new meaning.

I will never forget Tony's formula. It is as follows:

FOCUS—attention. PHYSIOLOGY—body reaction. MEANING—making sense.

Depending on what you focus on, you will form a new perception that will lead you to your own newly formed reality. It follows that if you are willing to focus your energy on something, it will come true—this is the divine nature of your being. This formula is applicable to everything: from the cellular level to the whole structure of the universe.

Exercise (you can do this or just imagine it):

Buy two flowery potted plants. Bring them home and attend to only one of them. Place one in a dark place and leave it there—no watering, no light, no care. Place the other plant in a sunny environment next to a window and water it every other day. In a week's time, compare the well-being of the two plants. Obviously, one will wither away while the other flourishes.

This simple experiment confirms two things:

1. Everything in the universe is interconnected: for our plant, it is the water and sunlight, cooperation vs. competition (the pot plant is not fighting or competing with the sun or the water, they all are working together).
2. You will either flourish or perish, depending upon where your energy focus is placed. Ignore it and it will go away. No focus, no energy—no life.

"Concentrate all your thoughts upon the work at hand. The sun's ray does not burn until brought to a focus." Alexander Graham Bell

CHAPTER 5

Relationships and Perceptions: Conversation with a Monk

My trips to the Benedictine community at New Norcia are always amazing; they seem veiled in a mystical ambience. This visit was no exception. I came to see Father Anscar in particular. It's so lovely to see him. Our friendship is growing. I really don't know how to thank him for his generosity; the time he so graciously spends with me and the wisdom he so generously shares. At the end of my last visit, I gave Anscar a St. Benedict's medal. I bought this medal in Subiaco, Italy two years prior while visiting the Benedictine monastery in Tuscany. The significance of the medal is that it is from the monastery founded by St. Benedict himself six hundred years ago. Anscar is of course a Benedictine monk, too. He was so thrilled! Although he is seventy-six years old, his eyes lit up and he kissed the medal, showing his genuine childlike spontaneity. It was a joy to see his youthful aura.

By 8 a.m., the monks have already prayed three times: at 5:15, 6:45, and during the morning mass at 7:30. So this time I didn't miss a beat, I prayed together with the monks "religiously" every prayer time. It is an amazing experience. It is peaceful, calm, and profound. The monks are singing the psalms. There is a rector, or leading voice, usually Father David. So he gives the key cue and the monks join in with the singing. There is also young Robert, a novice who has been at the monastery for the past nine months. His job is to play the organ situated at the back of the chapel near the entrance. Before he joined the monastery he played in a jazz band.

As the monks sit in the chapel across from each other, the wooden floor of the main aisle is all that separates them. There are usually four monks in the pews on one side of the aisle and four or five on the other. This creates two sets within the choir. When singing psalms, they compliment each other—the group on one side singing one part and those on the other chiming in. It works in perfect harmony. Visitors like me can join them, too. There is a music sheet provided so anyone can join in on the singing and praying with the monks. It's enchanting.

That morning, after I'd attended the morning prayers and enjoyed my continental breakfast at the guesthouse, Anscar was waiting for me outside near my car, just as we'd agreed last night. I arranged my overnight stay with the ever-smiling Julie, the guesthouse desk manager, and walked outside. Anscar was standing there right in front of my car, but at first I didn't recognize him. He was not wearing his usual black habit. Now he was wearing dark pants, a green sweater, and a blue hat with "Australia" embroidered in white letters around the base. Only Anscar's familiar voice told my mind to recognize my friend: the power of perception—how amazing!

It is a perfect example of the fact that we don't really see with our eyes, we see with our brains (minds). Our brain tells us about the world based on what it already knows and is used to, and not the true reality. Only after encountering something familiar—like the sound of Anscar's voice—does the brain start sorting through the memory file to find the familiar link and make the connection. What is even more remarkable is that I can reflect on it right now and talk about the behavior of my own brain through that same brain.

This is the mystical power of the brain.

We get into my car and drive about a kilometer down the road and then we turn left into another. We drive for about three more kilometers and then Anscar directs me to turn right into a red gravel road that leads into the bush. We stop to open a wire gate that is normally closed to the public (we are still on the monastery's land). We drive through knee-high grass. I am thinking that my car is a typical city vehicle (without four-wheel drive) and although a diesel, not designed for off-roading in the bush. Anyway, we proceed and I use mainly first gear to make sure we don't get bogged down. Soon we hit another gravel road that leads to another wired gate. We pass through and continue our journey. Going up a hill, we find ourselves in the middle of the Aussie bush. Suddenly Anscar exclaims, "We are here!"

We disembark and Anscar leads me deeper into the bush. Almost as if by lifting a curtain, right in front of my eyes appear these unusually tall grass trees, and they are everywhere. It seems as if the whole family of them is living here. I've seen grass trees before, however, they are usually fairly short—about one to one and a half meters (three to five feet) tall. Not these giants.

Anscar leads me to the one he wants to show me. It's roughly five to five and a half meters tall—*that's nearly eighteen feet!* This is an extraordinary sight. I've never seen anything like it and I'm sure not many others have either. Anscar tells me that the grass tree grows about an inch a year on average, while slower-growing species might not even reach half that amount. Really? I make quick calculations and confirm that the giant grass tree standing serenely in front of me has been here for centuries! How is that possible? This is a living tree; it has green leaves! How has this grove of grass trees—and this majestic old chieftain—survived the bushfires and the parrots that delight in dining on these trees (evidence of which can be seen all around here)? I take a deep breath. I take a photo with my iPhone. I marvel. I take some more photos. I am spellbound.

Anscar is visibly excited. We proceed to mingle among the grass trees of different shapes and sizes. Alongside them we see clusters of beautiful flowers of the most vivid hues gazing up at us as if to say, "Welcome, friend." Anscar intuits my thoughts and remarks, "You see Mirek, they knew you were coming, so they all came out to greet you!" It was one of the nicest things I've ever heard in my life. I look around and see an explosion of colors and shapes of bush flowers, like nature's own fireworks display. The colors range from bright yellow to deep blue, from white to purple to green—and everything in between. The incredible shapes and traits of the flowers are reflected in their names: the "Star of David" or the "yellow everlasting" that retain their brilliant, sunny color for years after they've been picked and brought home. It's a mystical place, no doubt!

As we venture deeper into the bush amongst the trees and

flowers, tall grass, and kangaroo droppings, we chat. I ask Anscar to look at the colors of the flowers through my Serengeti sunglasses. I tell him that these lenses are being used by astronauts to cut down on the glare and reflections to allow the viewer to see the world as it is. He looks at the flowers through my lenses and affirms, "Yes, they are even prettier now."

I take this opportunity to continue our conversation and ask my companion, "Do these flowers still blossom even when we aren't looking?" He replies, "Of course." I press him: "Yes, but you just said that these flowers all came out just for me today. Doesn't this mean that if no one is looking at them, they are not bursting with the joy of their colors?" When I put this timeless conundrum to Father Anscar, I was thinking about the quantum physics proposition that holds that particles behave differently when someone is observing them than when no one is watching (the famous double-slit experiment confirms this). I continue, "Is it not true that all we see is appearing only because we perceive it through our senses? Therefore, nothing really exists at all if there is no one to perceive it: no senses—nothing to receive ..." Anscar replies stridently, "They are here always *for the glory of God!*" He adds, "The little flower that is growing on the tip of the steep rocky mountain, where there is absolutely no access to anyone, it grows for the glory of God." Wow! Now I get his drift. This is my epiphany! In the absence of any human senses, there is always someone watching—God is always watching over His creation.

If this is not proof of the existence of God, I don't know what is!

When approaching experiments addressing the reality of the universe, every scientist must take into consideration all of the possible variables. Otherwise, if the scientist consciously omits certain available facts (or hunches), the experiment will be biased rather than objective. In the experiment about the origins of the universe, two suppositions must be considered: either the universe came about spontaneously without cause, or God is the creator of the universe.

So when Anscar says that the creation exists whether anyone is looking or not and it is because there is always someone looking, he is right. He is right because unlike scientists he is also taking into consideration another important factor—God. The Creator is looking at His creation; therefore, the colorful flowers are always there for the glory of God! This is not simply religious rhetoric—it just makes sense. Max Planck, the father of quantum physics, was a staunch scientist; nothing but scientific proof would satisfy him. When he received his Nobel prize for discovering quantum physics he explained that there is no doubt that there is something outside of all matter that causes the matter to form and operate in the fashion that it does: "All matter originates and exists only by virtue of a force which brings the particle of an atom to vibration and holds this most minute solar system of the atom together. We must assume behind this force the existence of a conscious and intelligent mind. This mind is the matrix of all matter."

The Dalai Lama's recent visit to Emory University in Atlanta shows that many people of all cultures are awaking to the flow of bridging between cultures. Briefing his audience on his project introducing Western science into Buddhist monastic education across Tibet and elsewhere, he explained: "It is quite a rich material about what I call the inner world. Modern science is very highly developed in matters concerning the material world. These two things separately are not complete. Together the inner and the external world are complete." The university will pay $700K for the tuition of the monks who then go back to their monasteries to teach Western science.

Brain cells: How many do we need?

My good friend Anscar said he sometimes meets people who don't remember what they've said, so they repeat themselves. One of these was an unfortunate friend who was suffering from dementia. At that moment, I could see that Anscar might be thinking about his own memory, although despite his age (he is in his late seventies) his mind is as sharp as a razor and he is always quick with a joke. We also spoke about the nature of our brains. We have around fifty to eighty trillion cells in our bodies and they are completely replaced every seven years. Remarkable. However, we are actually losing around ten thousand cells every day once we pass the age of thirty. It seems like a lot, but it is insignificant in comparison to what's left. Why is this happening? Is this a good thing or bad thing for us?

The good news is that Mother Nature is purposely diminishing the number of cells in our body (this includes our brain cells) for our own good. Because we have fewer cells, the remaining cells are compelled to make more and better connections between themselves, between neurons. When we are young, all of the cells are clustered together with little meaningful connection between them. It's a massive soup of cells, and they tend to be confused about their purpose. This is probably why we say, "youth is wasted on the young." Our youth is spontaneous and sometimes even crazy, daring, unpredictable—we believe we are invincible. It's all due to that chaotic soup of strong cells that interact with one another with little or no meaning. This is why young people need to have good coaches and mentors if they dream of ever succeeding. They all have an amazing potential, but without direction their potential is squandered. On the other hand, older people can learn to be more conscientious, steadier, and more thoughtful. Older people have fewer neurons (nerve cells), however those cells have better, stronger, and more well-developed and well-established connections between themselves. The support system of the cells is stronger and more efficient. This could explain why older ("nontraditional") students are doing so much better at university compared to their younger counterparts. It seems that as we age, the key to our wisdom comes from better, more useful connections within our brain system. And despite the energy and potential of the younger generation's vibrant brain cells, their brains are no match for older, more refined brains, grounded in experience. Simply put, there are few sages among twenty-year-olds!

An awareness of each person's individual perception is the key to communication between people. We all are subject to our own unique worldview. Our perception has been developing as our brains are exposed to the environment in which we grew up. Our perceptions began taking shape while we were interacting with our parents, then our schoolteachers, and our peers—even the climate and geographic location has a profound impact on our perception and view of the world.

In my practice, clients who experience issues revolving around relationship difficulties quickly learn that the source of their unresolved disagreements often lies in lack of relating to the other person's perception. I asked one client, "If your relationship was a color, how would you describe it?" Her description of the meaning of color was very different from her husband's perception. For her, the color yellow represented a boring and flat relationship, while he thought that yellow signified happiness and stability. For her, the color yellow was negatively charged, while for him it was quite positive. Researchers confirm that we all perceive colors slightly differently. It is because we don't really see through our eyes but with our brains, and our brains are wired for individual perception. Only by identifying each other's needs can communication become effective and contribute to an improved relationship. There are different ways to resolve conflict, but by enquiring with intention to understand the other person's views and individual perceptions we are getting off to a good start.

CHAPTER 6

Modern Mysticism in Therapy

In the course of researching the role of mysticism in counseling, I conducted interviews with therapists who have encountered "the mystical" in their practice. They reported remarkably similar themes. Each described the phenomenon as being real. Their names have of course been changed.

The mystical relationship between God and man

"Bob": An urge to follow God

"When I would talk about [my mystical experience] afterwards, I felt that there was one thing that was God. There was oneness to everything; that permeated all reality and it led me to choose to get baptized".

"Michael": Union with God through creativity

"I think it's our fundamental nature to be creative. I see that in clients, when they move through a certain amount of therapeutic work and they become more creative just in the way they live. A lot of sacred traditions talk about people being 'made' in the image of God, and quite often God is referred to as 'the creator.' I see our role as being creative as well."

"Nick": Making space for God

"Willingness over willfulness. So ascetic personalities will fast in order to empty themselves of the false self to make more room for God or the divine, whereas the therapeutic idea of fasting is what you do before you go in for an operation."

The therapeutic relationship and ways to happiness

"Michael": Awareness—mind, body, spirit

"From talking to traumatized clients and seeing their dissociation from their body, from their emotions, and from their cognitive dysfunction, I'm always trying to work with them to help them have a different experience of themselves, a more consolidated one. I am always inviting them to bring their awareness back—I ask, what's happening with your feelings? Are there any particular thoughts to lead them away to a heightened experience of themselves?

"Bob": Mystical experience as a means of connection

"I started to pray with a client. If I had not had that mystical experience through prayer, I wouldn't have been praying with that client. But what that experience gave me was a sense that God sees us with pure love, that he's willing to forgive us, and really just loves us—and doesn't, you know, want to smite us or whatever [laughs], but also that you can start afresh, and for me, that really informs my life."

"Nick": Relationship as a fundamental ingredient

"A lot of psychotherapeutic techniques don't teach relationship, they teach technique and that's an instrumental approach to psychology. In fact, lots of people are really seeking relationship. Now if you use a Christological approach to that, Christ was all about relationship, completely about relationship, and the right view of relationship with the person and the divine."

"Michael": Metaphysical interests

"I think it's important to make space for clients to bring in any metaphysical questions or interests they may have—whether religious, more generally spiritual, or secular. Because for many they're extremely important and can easily get overlooked."

"Paula": Sensitivity

"I experience the mystical every day. I'm sensitive to beauty that presents itself all around me all the time through simple things. I also use prayer."

How spirituality and mysticism are practiced

"Nick": Encountering the mystery of God

"That's what Christ was really talking about. Drop it, just drop it; do it the moment you've got the opportunity to drop whatever you're attached to. That's how you'll enter the kingdom.

"Yeah, surrender, just get rid of it. Drop it. Have you ever noticed that when kids are crying and you want to get them to stop, you'll do something really funny and all of a sudden they just drop it. There are still little tears running down their cheek, but they've moved on. It's gorgeous just to see a little kid do that.

But adults don't do that. We harbor resentment—I think that's what Christ's talking about. So the spiritual life is really leading to what some theologians call the "second innocence," the awe and wonder of God, the full wonder of Christ. You transcend all this muck and bullshit and see that it's all good, it's all part of this divine nature in God. Now *that's* mystic!"

"Paula": Awareness—being in tune

"My experience is that mysticism is external. It comes from the divine and its being channeled through the mystic."

"Michael": Transpersonal experience

"So that would be a fundamental aim of mine: to help them reconnect with their body, because through their body and in their body they can actually move their energy, even their energy centers. They sometimes glimpse moments of more integration or wholeness or completeness or satisfaction. It helps them step out of their awareness and their anxieties, and that gives them great hope, which adds a lot to the therapy.

"I believe, that on a spiritual or transpersonal level there's some sort of directional guidance or something being offered that will be helpful to people who are too anxious or apprehensive to notice, so when they get back in touch with their body it changes the state they're in to a calmer, more balanced state."

"Nick": An essential relationship

"Christ is in all people. So if you see it with the right eyes, you can have those experiences without any problem. Sufi mysticism speaks of it. You can find it in love making, you'll definitely find it playing music with other people."

"Nick": Focus on content vs. context

"How much do you like your therapist? Do you think the therapist has a genuine concern for you? And how much do you feel that that concern has an element of hope in it? Do you have a sense of warm regard for this person, and do you think the therapist has a sense of warm regard for you? It's in that relationship that researchers found that the higher the reliance between client and therapist, the greater the outcome. Which actually means that what really works in therapy is *how* things are delivered not *what*. It's not the content, it's the context."

Mystical experience: case studies

"Bob": Life-changing experience

"One woman disclosed that she had had a near death experience, but she hadn't even told her family because she didn't have confidence they would think she was sane or whatever.

"She said that during the vision, she was met by some lawyers in pinstriped suits. I don't think she had any deeply held religious beliefs because often they are the things that people describe—such as being met by Jesus or being met by previous family members and so on. And since she didn't have anything like that to guide her, it was almost like, you know, being met by lawyers or suits would make it very formal and secure. And obviously and they were informing her that she was to go back, that it wasn't her allotted time to pass.

"As a result of this experience, she changed her life direction and went from someone who was quite comfortable living a rather sheltered existence—what you might consider a 'normal' life in a small town doing accounting or something like that—to something a little bit different."

"Michael": Life-changing experience

"I'm thinking of a woman I was working with who was very stressed. Her relationship had broken up and just everything was difficult. She was very distraught. And I think it was our second or third session. She seemed to feel very safe working with me. And she kept saying 'I feel like there's something I need to know. There's something I need to experience. I don't know what it is. Like something's trying to tell me something.'

"And so she was quiet for a very long time. And then gradually tears started coming down her face. And of course I wanted to know what was happening but I kept quiet. She said that in that time she felt that the spirit of the three children that weren't born came to her one by one. It was very moving.

"And she said that each one said that it was OK, and she felt them actually touch her and she could feel them touching her skin. She even opened her eyes a bit to make sure that no one was touching her externally. And she was in a state of incredible bliss. And she felt after that, all her problems had just fallen away. It was very transformational.

"It really changed her life. So her hunch that something or someone was trying to communicate with her was correct, and she just needed that support and feeling of safety to listen.

"I would call that a mystical experience that had a very positive transformational outcome. You know she was completely functional afterwards. If it was some sort of psychotic thing she might have been all over the place, but she was very calm and clear and focused."

How did you experience the phenomenon and how did it influence you?

"Bob": Perception of wholeness and union

"The purest, purest love is the only way I can describe it. And there was nothing verbal. I didn't hear a thing, but something—through this love—something was speaking to me, saying that this is how I see you, this is how you are, you are perfect to me. Like how you see a newborn—how beautiful and innocent it is—that's how you are to me. You are just that beautiful and that special and I love you. That's the only way I can describe it."

"Michael": The mystical is spontaneous

"The more I can step back, the more the client can come forward into their experience. But there's an active role going on; the therapist must remain attentive, but not take any action. If a client said, 'I'd like to have a mystical experience,' it would be like *wow!* The pressure's really on now. Because we can't manufacture it—it has to happen on its own."

"Paula": Another level of consciousness

"I was initiated into a spiritual practice. My teacher went into a trance. I was alone in this room with him; it was very confronting. I was designated to 'hold the space,' but not what we call in counseling 'holding the space'—it was something much, much more profound, on another level of consciousness. My teacher went into what felt like an open tunnel. I felt that I had to be there 'to hold the space' for him to be able to come back. This doesn't happen all the time, but when it does, it stands out."

Can anyone be a mystic?

"Bob": Everyone has the capacity

"Absolutely. I think we are all mystics. I think that's how we're made.

"It is almost like a radio frequency, that if we tune in to the right frequency or are on the right channel, then everything just aligns and we're connected, we're plugged in and switched on. We are a part of God, God is everything in us, and we are a part of that. But that becomes something that's greater than us as well."

"Nick": Everyone has the capacity

"We are all designed to be mystical beings—all of us. Everyone is a mystic. Well, *we are!* Because we are created in God. That's all. So all we're trying to do is see our right relationship with that. What is a saint, what is a mystic? A saint is a sinner that never gave up. [laughs] Isn't that right? I mean it's that simple. And that's bloody hard to do. Don't give up! Therese of Avila, says the worst thing you can do on a spiritual journey is not to fail. It's absolutely guaranteed that if you're going to pursue a journey toward mysticism or spirituality, you're going to fail. Absolutely. The worst thing to do is to give up."

The need for new consciousness and new directions

"Michael": Mystical as a necessity, not a luxury

"I think that mystical experiences—or feeling more connected with the divine—impact on our morality and how we live our life. In that sense I think it's very urgent at the moment, because there are lots of very prominent people who are seeing that. The way we are living, pushing to the extreme, is damaging things so much and at such an alarming rate.

"Working as a counselor for nineteen years, I would say that there has been an increase in interest in the mystical, and I wonder if that's not because of the urgency; there needs to be some sort of global transformation, a change of attitude. Its not just a luxury, it's a necessity."

"Nick": Returning to basics

"God is ever present, but we're not. Our modern culture teaches us how to run away from it and seek spirituality elsewhere. And that's why I'm very sad about the fact that our culture has not returned to its own traditions—it's our best chance of entering into the divine. We need to have the right relationship with nature, the right relationship with the technology of peace.

"It's about virtues, patience, temperament, and seeking to understand all these other things that we've lost because we're so focused on outcome we forget the process. Because we thought, 'bugger this, we don't need these virtues,' we're on a collision course between two sets of values, and one will have to give."

Relationship between science and mysticism

"Bob": Manifestations of ESP (extrasensory perception)

"The brain and our consciousness have a really strong parallel from my understanding, certainly. I know there's been work done on stimulating parts of the brain behind the temples that has induced experiences of the divine, and I know that people can experience a consciousness change from brain injury, and I'm familiar with Oliver Sacks and his work with brain-injured people, and so on. But there's also stuff that runs contrary to that as well, and I know there's been some research about near-death experiences, for one. I know examples in which people have experienced consciousness where there's been no brain activity, cases in which they've had treatment of aneurisms, or where they've had to have all their blood removed, and yet they've had some experiences of consciousness outside of their brain and their body or they have had our-of-body experiences. There are cases in which people have had vision restored or reanimated their body after clinical death. There could be a whole range of reasons why that could be the case.

"Obviously consciousness is not just the brain; our consciousness may also be connected in other parts of nature, whether it be other dimensions or whatever. Consider string theory and similar investigations into quantum physics ... Perhaps there are other ways that our consciousness could operate outside of our brains as well."

"Nick: Quantum physics reveals mysticism rather than inventing it

"Well my view about all of that is that Einstein didn't 'discover' anything, it was just revealed.

"So Einstein would be a mystic in the sense that he described how God works. The Christian mystic, Julian of Norwich, describes *why* God works as He does when she says, 'All shall be well, and all shall be well, all manner of things shall be well.' Her mystical theology is that all things get bounced back to God. Her mysticism was the result of a near-death experience; she spent the rest of her life meditating on and writing about her visions."

"Paula": Science does not interfere

"There is no need to be too scientific about it. Phenomenology is scientific enough and some people cannot be convinced, no matter what. There is a growing interest in the mystical, and that's very welcome."

Personal experience of the mystical

"Bob": God's forgiveness as mystical experience

"When I said the words, 'I ask you for forgiveness,' something in my conscience actually picked up and it was similar to that experience with Buddhism—let go of your attachments—and I went with it. I sort of thought, 'OK, yep, I do recognize what I was doing was wrong, and I'll stop doing it and ask for forgiveness about that sort of thing.'"

"Nick": Mysticism as a penetration of God's reality

"God isn't just all sweetness and light. This is what the Spanish mystic, John of the Cross, was talking about: God's being is so dark, it is like a dark light. He said the dark night is like a dark ray and it is so insurmountably mysterious, so unfathomably available that what God does is He empties us of ourselves in order for that dark ray to go through. Because God is so pure, oh so pure, He is pureness of being; any muck that's in the soul can really do a lot of damage, as God shines His dark light through you. So John of the Cross says that God purges the soul, cleans the soul of its human nature, or of its falseness, so God can reside in the person.

"I think mysticism to me is the ultimate penetration of God's reality in you. That's what mysticism is. And its not necessarily a transcendent experience, it can be absolutely, utterly mundane. So my understanding of the 'mystical experience' in the Catholic mystical tradition is that it can operate, and best operates, while you're doing the dishes or washing the floors. True mysticism is the penetration of God's reality in the absolute commonplace of life. That's mysticism, in a sense of truly penetrating the reality of it, the beauty of it."

Summary

From the foregoing revelations, we can see that mysticism plays a role in establishing better communication in the counseling context and beyond. The sense of mutual intuition that all humans possess can help bond the client and the therapist in a meaningful alliance. The awareness of self and the mystical realm in a therapeutic relationship can be of significant assistance. Therapists who are committed to viewing their clients holistically allow intimate beliefs to surface and encourage the client to share their true self.

Mystical experiences need not imply religious beliefs on the part of the therapist or the client; an agnostic or atheist therapist can relate to the client by establishing a mutual understanding of what creativity, intuition, perception, or an insight represents.

CHAPTER 7

Overcoming Adversity

Grace was waiting for me in the café near the station. I was already about five minutes late. In the meantime she had ordered her favorite latte and sipped on it while looking over her notes on her iPad. I had promised to continue my story, with this installment covering my earlier life. She was preparing for her speech for the seminar and she wanted to talk about the influence of the younger years on later success. Grace had many resources to choose from, but she said I was her number one choice.

"I'm so sorry to keep you waiting Grace; I got stuck in traffic," I offered as I approached her table from behind. She turned and smiled. I sat down on the opposite side of the small round table. Then she responded, "Never mind, I just got here a few minutes ago and got myself a cuppa. Do you want your green tea?"

"I think I'll try the rose bud for a change; this is the only place in town that serves it so well—no, don't get up. I'll get it," I said. I stood and walked to the counter to order my brew. I returned with two glasses of water while waiting for my tea.

"What are your earliest childhood memories?" Grace enquired.

"My first and earliest memory was my mother reading fairy stories while she was bedridden, and then her passing and her funeral. I had just turned three. I remember the coffin in our house being positioned up too high for me to look inside," I explained. "In those days, you see, it was customary for the deceased to stay at home in an open coffin for a few days so the family and visitors could come and pay their last respects."

"It wouldn't happen today, I don't think," Grace said.

"I remember being quite small. Since I couldn't see my mum lying in the coffin, when no one was watching I pulled myself up by the coffin's edge to get a glimpse of my mum. She was lying there motionless, dressed in a black dress, her hands joined together as if she was praying. She had a black scarf on her head. I couldn't hang there for too long, so I would drop down on the floor and then try again. I did this several times.

"I also remember the vivid smell of the flowers that surrounded the room. To this day, when I walk into a florist the smell of fresh flowers instantly reminds me of my mother. It bothered me for many years, because I associated it with my mother being dead. However, since I decided that the smell of fresh flowers gives me a special connection with my mother, my view changed to the opposite. One day I decided to love everything about flowers—especially their smell. I have always had this feeling that my mother is present around me all the time, and the smell of flowers takes it to another level; the connection seems more tangible. I have kept fresh flowers in my home at all times ever since."

"Such a wonderful way to turn things around," Grace observed.

"This experience also helped me to help my clients. The idea came to me spontaneously while I was speaking with one of my clients. She was suffering terribly from missing her mother who had died years ago. She explained that she and her mum used to play piano together. The piano was still in her house after her mother passed away, but she couldn't bring herself to play it. Each time she heard the sound of piano, it brought sad memories. I proposed the possibility of changing the association between her mother and the sound of the piano. Instead of grieving over the happy times that cannot be repeated, I said, 'What if you look at the situation from a different perspective? What if the sound of the piano was the celebration of the times spent together?' I suggested she use the piano as a reminder about these wonderful feelings she was able to share and experience with her mother.

"It was quite amazing to see how her eyes suddenly brightened up," I continued. "Then she said, 'For years I've struggled with this sadness. I love my music, but I was not able to play the piano without feeling shattered. Now I can see the gift that my mother left behind, thank you.'

"She was clearly amazed at how a different way of looking at things can change the things you are looking at. The transformation was so sudden and visible that it almost seemed like a divine intervention. Such moments remind me of what a mystical experience looks like: an invisible connection, yet palpable and real. It makes us see that things are not as bad as they seem.

"Since my mother died when I was three, my father had no other option but to place me in day care while he was working. I was dragged from one day care to another. Some places I liked, some I didn't. It usually boiled down to who was running it. I can still smell the scent of the disinfectants that they sprayed those old buildings with! Sometimes when I watch movies featuring psychiatric asylums of the late nineteenth century, they remind me of those days long ago that were filled with terrible feelings of separation and suppressed emotions.

"I remember one day my father left me in one if those places. As soon as he dropped me off, I realized that something was missing. I started to panic; I was very upset and I cried all day long. No one knew what was wrong with me and I couldn't explain my frustration clearly enough to make them understand. I just kept demanding 'my friend.' The caregivers were puzzled; they kept bringing me all the other kids that stayed there, but I was inconsolable. When my father arrived from work late that afternoon, he immediately understood the reason for my distress: it was the stuffed toy I liked to suck on—I called it 'my friend.' Ha! It turned out that during the morning rush, my father simply forgot to pack the toy for me. I was so attached to 'my friend' that I didn't want to part with him ever! Not having my friend for the entire day was certainly a major crisis for me," I smiled.

"Who gave you the idea of calling your stuffed toy your 'friend'?" asked Grace.

"I don't remember; it could have been my father. Lots of kids have their imaginary friend, I suppose I needed something more tangible," I joked.

"My fixation with my friend lasted a long time, until one day when my brother who was nine years older than me got together with some of his buddies and decided to get rid of my friend. My brother's motivation to send my friend away was that he was embarrassed to walk with me in the park while I was chewing on my friend. By now I was four, and he thought it was way past time for me to be over such things. He explained to me why he was 'killing' my friend and then he lit it on fire and burned it up right in front of my eyes. I was shocked to the core!

"My brother and his friends laughed and I laughed with them with tears falling down my cheeks. I was afraid to upset my brother and his henchmen for fear that I might be next! I felt lost for some time afterward—I don't know long, but it felt like forever. Going cold turkey now without my friend was devastating—I was shattered. Gradually, my withdrawal symptoms subsided and I recovered completely.

"My brother's high jinks that day weren't his only mean-spirited games. I think the worst was when he and his friends decided to play with me like with a toy. I was around five, so they must have been around fourteen or fifteen—a pretty big age gap. My father sometimes left me under my brother's care because apart from day care there was no other alternative. My eldest brother Andrew was nineteen at the time, so he was usually away from home, out with his friends drinking in the nearby park," I explained.

"However, that particular day left me with a fear of heights for a long time. We were in our apartment, which was up on the fourth floor. We had a balcony looking out over the street below. On that day, one of my brother's friend was tossing me up in the air and catching me, the kind of thing you do to amuse a small child. But then the boy decided to go a step further with this amusement and see what my reaction would be if he dangled me over the safety railing of the balcony. He picked me up and held me in the air, fifteen meters above the street below. I was screaming my lungs out and wiggling my little body, but thank God he didn't drop me! The ordeal probably didn't last long, but for me time stopped, as I was consumed by fear—not so much paralyzed by it, as submerged in it. The boys were all laughing, including my brother. They probably thought that it was funny seeing me so scared," I related.

"That's so mean, you must have been scared to death!" Grace exclaimed.

"Yes, I know I was overjoyed when I was able to be in school rather than in day care or the 'care' of my brother," I reflected.

"I remember my time spent in school as an opportunity to fight with my teachers for my recognition and acknowledgement. As first it seemed like I could never do anything right. When I was a small child and first entered my local school, I was so excited and eager to learn. In the very first days of my primary education, my teacher set up a competition to earn a trophy for the best reader among all the kids from year one. Our class was quite large—forty-four students. We knew each other more or less from growing up in the same neighborhood, but this was something different. This was my first opportunity to begin my education from a good position.

"When the competition began, I was sure that I was going to win it; I was a very good reader. I practiced the material given to read at home until I almost knew it by heart. I was on fire!

"And sure enough, I was awarded a medal. The engraved letters on the face of the medal read, 'For excellent reading skills.' The medal was made of aluminum and it was attached to a red ribbon. The shiny medal and the red ribbon really stood out against my black school uniform," I recalled.

"I was so proud and happy! When I came home from school, I didn't want to take my uniform off. But nobody at home seemed to care. My stepmother wasn't keen on praise; she was much better at criticizing. She probably said something like, 'I wonder how long you'll wear it before you lose it.' I don't know if my father noticed my medal. I was happy anyway. I didn't care about her comments or anyone else's. I was eager to go back to school. I thought this school thing was going to be fun!

"The next day I was still buzzing with excitement. I don't recall that I did anything wrong in school that day, other than laughing a lot, as usual, and perhaps running around like a happy kid."

"Yes, I can imagine what an energetic child you must have been—you're still fireball!" Grace gently chided.

"I always felt that my teacher didn't really like me, but I never discovered the reason why, although I have my hunches. For one thing, she didn't like my father. My father was a foreman at the local factory. He worked there for forty years while the works changed hands from the Austrian occupiers through the Nazi overlords and finally, the postwar era of Soviet rule. My father was a committed employee and known as an exemplary specialist and everybody's friend. My teacher, who—judging by her Russian-sounding name and accent—was from the heart of the Soviet empire, did not approve of my father's proletariat background. This was a paradox because at that time, Poland was a Soviet-dominated Communist state, so my father's working-class background should have been in favor. Not with her. She was only interested in people who aspired to climb up through the ranks of the Communist party. She called them the 'intelligentsia,' but really they were just opportunists," I said without empathy.

"So as my primary school teacher didn't fancy my father, and she resented me, too. Throughout my first four years of school, she let me feel her resentment on a daily basis. I can't recall her ever acknowledging my progress, and she delighted in physical punishment. She always talked about this Soviet educator named Makarenko, who apparently favored disciplining pupils by inflicting physical pain. Her specialty was to pull my little nose and twist it sideways so hard that tears would well up in my eyes. She subjected me to this torture on a daily basis."

"Was this normal? Couldn't you have complained about this to your father?" asked Grace.

"No I wouldn't dare tell my father, he would have been angry that I gotten into trouble again. My father had faith in the educational system. He thought that a little discipline was warranted. I couldn't tell my father, so my teacher had a field day with me."

"That's so sad," Grace said.

Changing the subject, Grace said, "Tell me what happened on the day after you received your medal."

"Yes, this was a most significant day. It remained in my psyche for the rest of my school days," I said with disappointment in my voice.

"So, on that day my teacher pulled me aside and in front of the whole class. She removed my precious medal, saying, 'I am taking this medal away from you as a punishment for behaving badly.'

"I thought, *what?* I was traumatized by this unjust action. I was humiliated in front of my class and punished most severely. I couldn't see the link between my behavior—which only amounted to laughing and running around like most kids do—and stripping me of my greatest achievement in life! My whole world collapsed under the weight of my disappointment. I was dumbfounded.

"I was afraid my father would be angry at me if he found out that I was punished for bad behavior again. I concluded that the teachers and school were my number one enemy. I felt like quitting school altogether and running away to my mother's arms, though I didn't know where she was. So I swallowed my grief and walked slowly back to my desk. I remember being devastated.

"I was accustomed to making these kinds of snap judgments. When my mother died, I felt that I was on my own. My father was very caring, but he never really understood me. No matter how hard he tried, he could never be my mother. I was growing up in my own world. I had to make quick decisions about who was a friend and who was a foe.

"So I decided: school was for fun, and the learning part was optional. I've got to watch out for teachers, as they are probably not my friends. I gave myself advice: go and have fun while you're in school. And I stuck to that advice. For me school was fun, fun, fun. I got myself into trouble many times, but always managed to come out unscathed. Looking back, I know I was a capable kid, and I always did enough work to get me through. My fun was a happy kind of fun. I always got a kick out of making the whole class laugh—even the teachers sometimes laughed with me.

"This attitude lasted until I graduated from high school. Then I went to several different post year twelve schools mainly just for fun. Shortly after my arrival in Australia, I entered university to pursue medicine and stayed there for two years until I discovered I had a knack for sales—and I had a young family to support. So it wasn't until I turned forty-four that I finally went back to school. I was so excited about learning again that I stayed for five and a half years of full-time study, earning two degrees.

"When they called my name at my graduation, I went up on the stage, grabbed a microphone—though graduates were not supposed to speak—and to the dismay of the professors, parents, and graduates, I declared, 'I lost my interest in school at the age of six, however, today the tide is turning.' Then I made a gesture as if I was drawing a bow and shooting arrow into the sky. The whole crowd erupted in cheers. I thought to myself: *Now, after all these years, I've earned my medal back!* I was elated. I had bounced back, and making a hundred and eighty-degree U turn, I had succeeded!

"This moment in which I reclaimed my medal was purely mystical."

CHAPTER 8

Ancient Wisdom Connection: Aristotle on Happiness

Aristotle had a great capacity to examine and reflect upon his observations. His life was preoccupied with inquiring into the science of the human existence, its meaning and its purpose. Aristotle lived three and a half centuries before Jesus Christ's ministry, and he was therefore unaware of the Christian teachings that followed. However, the ethical norms and reasoning that evolved through Christ's teachings are remarkably similar to those of Aristotle's teachings three centuries before. Aristotle would have had no idea that his deductively valid arguments and prescription for attaining true happiness would go hand in hand with the doctrine that influenced the Christian church since it's inception. Aristotle's inspiration produced countless talented theologians and philosophers, including distinguished thinkers such as St. Augustine and St. Thomas Aquinas, whose profound works on human spirituality and reason have substantially contributed to our modern understanding. Their respective works shined a light on the question of the relationship of God and man that intrigues and continues to inspire modern existential and spiritual thinkers.

Aristotle argued that humans are part of the "bigger plan" (in which we simultaneously belong to the universal family of all creation), and that we must have ingrained and inherited meaning that drives us toward rediscovery of the true nature of our being. He observed that all things (not just living) have a purpose and are subsequently destined to fulfill some specific aim. This aim however, must be of some value or "good." He explained: a hammer is made for hammering, a knife to cut, an apple to be eaten, and a flower—as other living entities—to self-actualize. Consequently, humanity must also have been created with a certain function in mind. If God were the creator and universal source of love and happiness, then He would also equip humans with the capacity to attain some "good." And because man is created in the image of God, humans must reach out for not just ordinary good but for the ultimate, the highest, good.

Aiming for the highest good

What then could be the highest possible good for the human person? Aristotle implied that just as the flower or the frog naturally strives to achieve the optimum self-realization, so too humans must follow suit. The flower should not be fully satisfied to become just an average flower; it must strive to become the best flower possible. This requires some effort, in fact a lot of effort, conquering adversaries of changing weather or a hostile environment. A good example is the grapevine. The vine produces the best fruit only if it is threatened by the possibility of premature dying, thus preventing it from achieving full self-actualization. So the crafty vine tender will purposely deprive the vine of water and nutrients and expose it to the harshest environment (within limits of course). Only then will the vine produce, as if the last breath of life, the most beautiful fruits that in turn produce the best wine. It is the same with humans. As the Beatles sang: "It's getting hard to be someone, but it all works out." Hence, some suffering is a requisite part of the quest for attainment of the higher good. What is the "highest good" then? Is it material?

Aristotle's quest led him to the discovery that the highest good cannot be material. If it were, it would be easily attainable and naturally followed by a hunger for more. This is the case with pleasure. How often do people confuse *happiness* with *pleasure*? The fundamental difference lies in the spiritual nature of happiness. It is well known that money and material possessions do not offer a sustainable source of happiness. Money can make people happy—especially those who do not have it. The hunger for more money, more toys, more luxuries can easily become an addiction, like gambling or other soul-destroying activities. Warren Buffett, one of the richest people in the world, was once asked this same question: Is there a limit to how much money one can spend or how many luxuries one can amass? He answered that there are millions of millionaires in America today, and they enjoy a similar luxury lifestyle to billionaires. Buffett quipped that he can only live in one house at the time and drive his favorite car.

People living in the first world enjoy an unprecedented level of comfort and prosperity. Yet, the poorest societies—such as the indigenous South American peoples or other societies not participating in these booming economies seem to be the happiest ones. Statistically, major depression and suicide rates among the populations of the developed world are alarmingly high, while these problems are rare in "underdeveloped" societies.

Something is missing! Material goods offer a kind of transitory happiness; it is short lived and unsustainable. Aristotle observed this phenomenon almost twenty-five centuries ago. It is startling that after all this time we have made very little (if any) progress. Aristotle assured us that there must be a better way to achieve happiness, and if it is not material, it must come from the soul—from the inside out, rather than the other way around.

Seeking deeper meaning

Aristotle noted that our human connection to the universal creation—the miracle of life itself—is not enough. The philosopher explained that the phenomenon of life is not exclusive to humans: animals, plants, insects—even bacteria—share the life force that binds us all together; still, this is not enough for man. According to Aristotle, man's natural attraction to God is most likely driven by the higher intellect, a gift exclusively given to humankind. The similarities between animals and us most likely lies in the longing to be in the company of those who are better, more skillful, or smarter than us. In the animals' case, this is probably for survival, as it is better to hang around those who are more skillful hunters, or those who can teach new skills. If certain skills cannot be effectively taught, then animals would increase their chances of survival by living together in mutually beneficial packs. This extends to domesticated animals as well. They not only seek out humans to keep us company (although that is a key part of our relationship), but being great observers, they learn a lot from us—as if trying to be more useful members of "the pack."

This also applies to our relationship with God. Man is drawn to God naturally. Since humans, with their God-given intellect and ability to reason, have been positioned at the pinnacle of God's creation, they find themselves at the top of the mountain, where the choice seems obvious: they reach for the limitless, and therefore God. It is a natural impulse. This also explains why the alternative—going downhill, or backsliding—is so undesirable for us. It follows that humanity must naturally yearn for this reconnection with a higher power.

Since man is so closely related to God, he must have been equipped with the intellectual capacity to establish spiritual kinship with his creator. Higher awareness demands greater responsibility; therefore, man has been entrusted with the highest duty of responsibility toward himself and God's creation.

Aristotle acknowledged this phenomenon and suggested that humans are expressly equipped to carry out special tasks that distinguish them from other living things. He added that before pursuing these challenges, humans must first be clear of all the obstacles that cloud the mind and body. That is, we must practice virtues that will lead us to the highest good for ourselves and others in our quest to attain the highest level of human functioning.

Eudemonia—the "highest good"

The famous Greek sage proclaimed that the only way to approach any meaningful undertaking is through practical application. He felt that to ponder concepts is fine, but if we want to accomplish anything, we must roll up our sleeves and dive in. Interestingly, this also applies to contemplation, which is the highest form of happiness (according to Aristotle). It might seem like contemplation is doing little, but even in contemplation diligent practice is necessary. Aristotle was concerned with finding the path that reveals the mystery of achieving earthly and everlasting prosperity of the soul: human flourishing, or *eudemonia*, as he called it—the "highest good."

Aristotle postulated that the human capacity for reason must be the key. However, in order to employ reason to ensure a flourishing life, one must practice a high degree of virtue. For Aristotle, only those who pursue impeccable ethical (moral) behavior are destined to achieve the highest degree of happiness. So saying, Aristotle implied that he discounts those who display extreme or harmful behaviors. For example, in the case of courage, excess is rashness and deficiency, cowardice. With respect to spending money, generosity is a mean between the excess of wastefulness and the deficiency of stinginess.

Aristotle rejected extremes and favored the behavioral middle ground in the attainment of a virtuous character. He was convinced that only under these circumstances could mankind achieve the highest good that nourishes the soul. Modern theology agrees: *spirituality doesn't arrive fully formed; it requires effort*.

Friendship is the way

Aristotle viewed friendship as an ideal means to form meaningful relationships. From the perspective of modern behavioral sciences, this postulate holds true. We are highly organized social beings; since the beginning of time, we have valued the power of working and playing together for mutual benefit. For example, it was more productive to organize hunting parties than to hunt alone. Throughout the ages, teamwork guaranteed better results, whether on a small or much grander scale. We can observe this in practice today when we see a well-run mom-and-pop restaurant or the amazing synchronization of a huge corporation, such as NASA, that can land a man on the moon. In both cases, the principal remains the same—cooperation is required to achieve great things. Just like our ancestors, we understand the value of friendship in achieving higher levels of success. Aristotle further refined this concept in *Nicomachean Ethics*. He felt friendship could be divided into three basic types:

1. Friendship based on pleasure
    (e.g., casual sex—emotionally driven, opportunistic)
2. Friendship based on utility
    (e.g., business relationships—*quid pro quo*)
3. Friendship based on virtue—the "perfect friendship," according to Aristotle

When psychologist Carl Rogers offers his person-centered, humanistic approach to counseling, or when Jesus proclaims that the greatest commandment is the one instructing us to "love thy neighbor as thyself," the Aristotelian concept of friendship based on virtue is at play. "For without friends," Aristotle insisted, "no one would choose to live, though he had all other goods."

Following Aristotle's deductive reasoning, if a virtuous life leads to attainment of the highest good, where the highest good represents the sustainable joy of life (not just temporary pleasures), then the ultimate destination for the human soul must be the state of happiness, in its highest and universally sustainable form.

So if the function of mankind is to attain eudemonia—good

life or happiness as the highest aim and purpose—*then the key is happiness that is derived from a virtuous and balanced life.*

As Aristotle himself concluded: "Happiness is the meaning and the purpose of life, the whole aim and end of human existence."

CHAPTER 9

My Father's Suicide:
An encounter with Dark Mysticism

We were cruising along the coast in a hired Mercedes convertible. I love that car. I have one at home, and I always hire one just like it when I'm traveling. Ever since I was seven years old, I dreamed that one day I would own one. Back then I would look at my black and white Mercedes advertising brochure over and over again. At that time, owning a Mercedes in Soviet-occupied Poland was an impossible dream. That car cost a million *zlotys*, the equivalent of a million dollars today.

I had already related a bit about my life and promised that I would provide more details one day. Luckily, this conference of mine helped us reconnect and I wanted to keep my promise. Grace believed I had so many stories to tell and she didn't want to miss anything. She thought this background would help her in writing her master's dissertation. I wanted to be of assistance, of course, and now she mentioned that she was preparing an essay on the subject of suicide. So I decided to share the details of my personal encounter with dark mysticism.

"Grace, I know that like me, you are interested in mysticism, but have you ever given much thought to 'dark mysticism'? You know, the idea that spirituality may not always be happy and joyous; that pain and suffering also has a place in our psyche or our souls—the concept of *malum in Deo*, the existence of evil.

"Yes, I'm familiar with the dilemma of good *and* evil as spiritual experiences. I assume you're referring to the unresolved question that bothered theologians and philosophers for centuries, yes?" I nodded. "Augustine and Aquinas spent their lives debating this issue," she continued. "I'm not particularly philosophically inclined, but I do sometimes wonder why bad things happen to good people. Why is there so much pain and suffering in the world, and where does evil come from? Why would a benevolent God who is omniscient and omnipotent allow suffering to exist?" she asked sincerely.

"Yes, it's a mystery to me, too. I often encounter this phenomenon in my therapy practice: good people experience incredible pain and suffering. I can't explain it. Early mystics, such as St. John of God or Theresa of Avila, talked about dark mysticism at length. For me, the closest I've come to experiencing dark mysticism was my father's suicide."

"Your father committed suicide?" she gasped. "I'm so sorry—I didn't know ... "

"Thanks. It was a very long time ago, when I was quite young. It's strange; his suicide gave me a different way of looking at my life that I never would have known otherwise. As tragic as it was, I somehow grew from the experience. Sometimes I reflect and find the meaning of it all. As a counselor, I understand that anxiety and even grief can motivate people to lead better lives. The pain can empower or paralyze us—it can destroy us, if we let it. It all depends how we view the event and how much support we are receiving. I feel that as a professional, I am better equipped to deal with my clients' suicidal ideation, as well as how it affects those around them. Yes, there is meaning in all of our life events. We may not realize it at first, but even tragic events can turn into new opportunities. It certainly turned out to be true for me."

Grace ventured somewhat tentatively, "What happened in your father's case? If you don't mind talking about it, that is."

After a moment of uncomfortable silence, I continued. "I didn't understand what was happening to my father. Several months before his death, he started acting strangely. He seemed to be preoccupied with distant thoughts. He worried about everything—whether there would be enough heating in the house for Christmas, or that we might suffocate if the windows were not opened to let more air in—trivial stuff. He was having really depressive thoughts, but back then I didn't know what 'depression' was."

"One day my father collapsed in front of me and started to cry uncontrollably. I was shocked. He just kept saying, "Everything is going bad." I didn't know what to do; I'd never seen my father in such a state. He had always been happy and cheerful person, full of optimism and energy.

"I improvised by trying to comfort him; I just started reassuring him and hugging him. I told him that things weren't so bad and that everything would be all right, that there was nothing to worry about. I told him this because I really thought that's how it was—from my perspective, anyway. Looking back, I realize that this event might have been a foreshadowing of my future as a professional therapist. In fact, part of my daily therapy work nowadays is lifting my clients from their distress or depression and pointing them in an alternate direction.

"Not long before this, my father had been forced to take early retirement. However, he was not happy to be at home all the time. The previous forty years of work gave his life so much meaning, but now he didn't know what to do with himself. He spiraled into an uncontrollable depression. He went to the psychiatrist and was prescribed medications that only made him worse. At the time, I didn't understand what was happening to my father or how to help. Why was he acting so strangely? He often talked about how he would have to leave everything behind soon. I know now that he was suicidal, but back then I didn't realize that the forthcoming tragedy was inevitable.

"I will never forget that horrible day. I was only three months into high school. My classes were all in the afternoon. My father left home in the morning, apparently to go shopping. However, he came back a half-hour later with nothing and looking confused. I saw him take a light leather belt that was hanging near the door. I was surprised to see the belt in this odd place, but I didn't think much of it at the time. Now I know he must have planned this. He picked up the belt and stared straight at me. His face looked troubled. It seemed like he wanted to say something. His eyes appeared hazy and confused. He hesitated. We were standing about five meters apart. We looked at each other for what seemed like a long time, though it was actually just a few seconds. I didn't realize it would be the last time I saw my father alive.

"For many years I blamed myself for 'letting him go' then. He looked at me the last time, slowly closed the door behind him, and disappeared. I had watched him walk through that door many times before, but this time my father wasn't coming back. I was the last family member to see him alive.

"When my father didn't return for several hours, my stepmother ordered, 'Go and find your father,' as if she was anticipating trouble. I had no idea what she meant or where I was supposed to look for him. My stepmother, whom my father married thirteen years after my mother died, had a domineering attitude toward everybody, but I always thought she aimed it at me in particular."

"What were you feeling?" asked Grace, who was sitting quietly and taking notes.

"I felt worried and sad. I didn't know what to do. I was kind of scared."

I turned to Grace remembering the event clearly. I must have looked worried because Grace said reassuringly, "It's OK, it's not happening any more."

"I went looking for him," I continued. "I went downstairs and as I was about to leave the building I placed my hand on the handle of the door that led into the cellar's long corridor. Something stopped me from opening that door. I was paralyzed with fear. I didn't know why, but I was afraid of what was behind that door. For many years I had nightmares about that place and that dreadful moment. I did not open that cellar door; instead, I quickly left the building feeling a sense of terror.

"Later, when the coroner completed his report, it became apparent that at the time of my hesitation my father was indeed in the cellar carrying out his suicide. He hanged himself with the belt he picked up earlier. He fastened the belt into the wooden bars of the door to our cellar unit. He wrapped the belt around his neck and let his body weight pull him down." I paused to collect myself.

"The autopsy confirmed that my dad had struggled," I said. "There were heavy marks on his neck made by his fingernails from where he had desperately tried to free himself from the noose that tightened around his throat. His oxygen-deprived body would not let him pull himself up and recover. Sadly, it was too late. Oh, God! There was nobody there to help him," I exclaimed. "But even as I stood outside the cellar door, I could not hear a sound—our cellar unit was too far from the main door.

"It is now clear that the evil of depression that he suffered pushed him over the edge and into the void of no return. All life abandoned him. The coroner's report confirmed that my dad died a slow, excruciatingly painful, and lonely death."

I pulled over and stopped the car. I had to step outside and get a breath of fresh air. I couldn't speak any more, not now anyway. It had all happened thirty-one years ago, but the grief never seemed to go away. The haunting memory of my father's suicide still provokes profound grief in me. Grace didn't say a word; it was all self-explanatory.

Assessment and observations

I've met many people in my practice who have attempted suicide. My own observations suggest that nobody really wants to die. There are of course exceptions; for example, individuals who suffer prolonged severe chronic pain or debilitating and incurable disease. Naturally, these people want to stop the pain at all costs. Whether the pain is physical, emotional, or psychological doesn't matter. Pain is pain and some people will tolerate pain better than others. However, I believe that if the pain can be mitigated or the individual's attention can be diverted elsewhere, suicide will lose its appeal in favor of the desire to live.

Depression can push anyone beyond the limits of despair. When the pain became too heavy to bear and there was no one to turn to who would acknowledge his pain. In this case his father opted for the only solution that his depressed and lonely mind could conceive—suicide. He lost the sense of meaning. He had been unhappy for a considerable time. He could live without happiness—he could get used to it, but without meaning, he could not progress. For him there was not much point in living, and there was nobody around to help him reclaim that sense of purpose, that drive he needed most.

Drawing on my case files, it is clear that reasons for attempting suicide vary considerably, depending on individual circumstances. There is usually more than one reason for considering suicide. It's often a cluster of events that accumulates over the years until it finally manifests itself in self-destructive thoughts. As reported, this case offers offers a perfect example: There were elements of the physiological, emotional, spiritual, and mental condition that contributed to the breakdown of the whole body system.

Physiological degradation

If you are exposed to a harmful physical environment for many years, your body reacts accordingly. If you smoke cigarettes, over time your body will suffer the ill effects of diseases that could lead to death. On the other hand, exercise, good diet, and lots of sleep promotes longevity.

On the physiological level, his father suffered from chemical withdrawal symptoms related to ingesting environmental toxins. He worked in a section of a factory that galvanized metal parts, so he was exposed to heavy metals and poisonous agents without wearing appropriate protection. For forty years his father was breathing in poison. During the war years and later during the Communist era, work safety regulations were nonexistent.

Pharmacological abuse

Today, it is all too common to be misdiagnosed and prescribed the wrong medication. We all dread it. However, it happens now and it was even more widespread in the past. It is therefore possible that his father was misdiagnosed or given some psychotropic medication that caused an allergic reaction. Such reactions can trigger suicidal tendencies. It is not difficult to imagine that when his father died in the early seventies, psychiatry in general and especially Communist state psychiatric knowledge was much less sophisticated than it is today. The error in diagnosing inappropriate or inadequate medications could have contributed to his father's death.

Emotional abuse

Emotional abuse can be triggered by many factors. Most of us have experienced emotional abuse of one type or another—whether at school, at home, or on social media, the opportunities abound. Sometimes siblings or even parents are the cause.

In this case his father after having lost the love of his life, his second marriage was another blow to his confidence and self-esteem. She often abused him emotionally by rarely acknowledging his presence or his many achievements. His need for significance and love and connection were shot. He was always very generous to others, yet he felt that he was surrounded by misfortune. Lack of support led him to believe that for him there was no room for growth, no meaning.

Spiritual disengagement

Many of us treasure our spiritual pursuits. Whether it's to honor traditions passed down through the generations, or simply for the sake of our personal growth, we take our spiritual lives seriously. We take pride in our spiritual beliefs and we stand ready to defend them. When our spirituality is threatened, we protest and defend it with all our might.

As reported, his father was a devout Catholic. Following his marriage to his second wife, he was denied the sacrament of Holy Communion. She was a divorcee and therefore his father was denied access to full participation in the life of church. It was important to him. For many Catholics, Holy Communion symbolizes unity with God and represents an extremely important link to God. To deny his father, a true believer and a follower of church doctrine, this sacrament was tantamount to spiritual estrangement.

This case is representative of the mystery of human existential struggles. He prayed frequently and lived an exemplary life. He would have hoped for God's grace that gives peace and prosperity to true believers—and his father truly believed. Like most believers he sought an intimate relationship with God, and he received it. But in the end, God's mystery was revealed to him through pain and disappointment. Was this a case of encountering dark mysticism?

So perhaps God is not always all light and happiness. There seems to be a type of dark mysticism, the dark side of the mystery of God, too. I don't know …

In many mystical religious traditions, God must be experienced tangibly. Sometimes this can mean that a life of suffering and pain has a purpose and is aimed at uniting with God. A mystical life also implies uncertainty and mystery. The mystical life is purportedly aimed at enriching and transforming a person's life. His father devoted his life to God, but he certainly didn't receive enrichment and transformation in the end. Could it be that his father experienced dark mysticism firsthand? Maybe he came too close to God's mystical spirituality. Whatever the case, during his spiritual breakdown, his body and mind succumbed to depression and took him away before his time.

Dealing with suicide

You might ask yourself: What would I do if confronted with the real possibility of a person I care about considering suicide?

Would I know how to help?

Here are some suggestions about how to approach a person manifesting suicidal tendencies based on my own observations in my practice. Don't pussyfoot around. Ask directly: Are you suicidal? Do you want to kill yourself? How far have you gone or how close have you come to killing yourself? Do you have a plan for how to kill yourself?

Have a normal, friendly conversation. Normalize the intentions of the person and talk about it, for as long as people talk meaningfully, nobody is in danger. By simply talking to the suicidal person, you will satisfy that person's most important need—acknowledgement and acceptance. Remember that the person is unwell and their thoughts are being distorted by the darkness of depression. The person believes (falsely) that their plan of suicide is the only logical solution. Although it may sound you like agreeing with the suicide, of course you are not. Yet, you must acknowledge the person in that moment. Your acknowledgement will satisfy their need to be respected, and reassure them that they are "sane." Any other approach, such as attempting to talk the person out of suicide or giving advice, is pointless. That's because it is not the suicidal person's reality at that moment—it's yours! So it follows that it is disrespectful. Who are *you* to give advice? Giving advice will *not* work in this situation. It will be viewed as an attack on their free will and dignity, and therefore, giving advice is condescending. It will only make matters worse.

Allow the person to have their say, even if it means you seem to be agreeing with the idea of suicide. It will defuse the tension. The suicidal person will gradually realize that they have a choice and nobody is going to alter their decision but themselves. It's a means of encouraging them to realize that in the end, they themselves must take responsibility for their final action; it's their choice, no one else will intervene. Not even God. Such intervention requires patience and calm, as your natural instinct will be to rush in and "save" them.

So what is suicide? Some researchers say it is an act of despair, a symptom of the unbalanced and depressed mind. The suicidal person is the subject of a vacuum, coming from a void that they are being sucked into against their will.

Physiologically, the depressed brain is deprived of the necessary ingredients for sustainability of the life force and happiness—dopamine and endorphins. Dopamine is a neurotransmitter that helps control the brain's reward and pleasure centers. Dopamine also helps regulate movement and emotional responses, and it enables us not only to see rewards but to also take action to move toward them. Endorphins are also neurotransmitters that carry electrical signals within the nervous system. Stress and pain are the two most common factors leading to the release of endorphins. Endorphins interact with the opiate receptors in the brain to reduce the perception of pain and act similarly to morphine.

A depressed person experiences depleted levels of these vital chemicals and is therefore in an altered state that prevents them from making any positive, life-affirming decisions. Nothing in the universe wants to die; all life forms want to grow and flourish. The flower wants to be the best flower that it can possibly be; it doesn't want to reach just half of its potential—no, the tulip, the rose, and the orchid all want to give the best before they die. This also applies to humans. We are part of the living world; we are part of the physical and biological reality. Therefore, a person who wants to kill himself is acting out of a kind of temporary insanity. The depressed person wants to stop the pain and is naturally acting egoistically. They don't consider how their suicide will affect others. Although they may fantasize about getting revenge for some perceived affront, the suicidal person doesn't clearly grasp that suicide is final. We are not programmed to contemplate death. Many of us (especially the younger ones!) think we are invincible and that death is something that only happens to others, never to us. This is an evolutionary survival mechanism. We are hopeful, and often believe that we will survive any circumstances and overcome any dangers. We are well aware from our observations that death is real, but since our subconscious can't grasp the concept of nonexistence, we subconsciously believe that death is happening to others, not to us.

The depressed subconscious mind thinks similarly: it is invincible and cannot die. So the depressed person might fantasize that after death they will be able to oversee their own funeral and watch others suffer or mourn for them. Unfortunately, there will be no satisfying revenge followed by a triumphant return to life once everyone has "learned their lesson." Death is final. In the dead brain there is no time or space for reflection, so the whole exercise is pointless.

If only the suicidal person was well informed and therefore able to stop and consider these few options, I suspect that many suicides would be prevented. Sadly, it is often too late for any intervention to prevent suicide. The downward spiral of depression fueling suicidal tendencies poisons the mind with dark, depressive thoughts and clouds the spirit with possessive emotions, inevitably leading the person toward the ultimate method of stopping the pain.

Fortunately, suicide is preventable.

Education is the key, for as long as the affected person is alive it's never too late. Often, individuals with suicidal ideation talk about it, sometimes between the lines. As a psychotherapist, I am sensitive to "hearing" that which is unspoken. However, this skill can be taught to anyone—just as first aid skills can be taught. Perhaps it's time to introduce suicide prevention first aid for everyone; it may save many lives.

There is light in the darkness. There must be purpose in every event, even the tragic ones. Sometimes I feel that my own experience with the awful reality of suicide drove me to become a counselor, an advocate for the prevention of suicide. Today, I know what to do; I cannot prevent suicide, but I can empower the individual with suicidal thoughts to stop and think—to reflect before taking that irreversible leap into the abyss. Consequently, I've been working with many suicidal clients, and I'm pleased to report that I haven't lost one yet. That doesn't mean I won't in the future, but so far I haven't.

It's clear that nobody wants to experience the deep darkness of losing a loved one. There's an old saying that "pain is inevitable, but suffering is optional." We will experience pain because it's a part of life. It all comes down to how we deal with pain. When a child falls and skins her knee, it hurts. However, once the abrasion is cleaned and dressed, it begins to heal. As long as the child knows she's being cared for, and that someone acknowledges her suffering, she soon forgets all about her pain. Children rarely revisit the source of their pain; they don't dwell on the past. They move beyond their scuffs and bruises, ready to engage in new adventures.

Tony Robbins, who is renowned for dealing with many suicide cases (among other successful interventions), said in a recent interview: "Pain can drive you or it can destroy you. We are made to make progress. Progress equals happiness. Progress makes you feel alive."

I believe there can be no progress without meaning. We cannot move forward toward any worthy goal if we have no clear direction. In his book, *Man's Search for Meaning*, psychiatrist and Auschwitz survivor Victor Frankl famously stated that "despair equals suffering without meaning," or rendered as an equation: $D = S - M$.

If only this message could reach out to those who suffer in despair, I am convinced that the suicide rates would fall dramatically.

If despair is preventable—and it is—then suicide is also preventable. Let's continue to embrace hope.

CHAPTER 10

Peter:
Conversation with a Professor of Theology

As a Christian, how do you explain to a non-Christian how Jesus can be divine and human at the same time?

"There are many ways to attempt to explain this but in the end the Church using philosophy and theology of different periods attempts to show that it is not illogical to hold that you can have two natures in the one divine person of Jesus Christ."

"Yes, it's a mystery. However, the New Physics proves it is possible that subatomic particles—like photons and biophotons, particles of light—being emitted from our human bodies, can have two natures: as particles or matter and as waves, all at the same time!" [This is noted in the discussion of the "double slit experiment" in Chapter 3.]

Correct me if I'm wrong, but we can't really talk about the true nature of God because we cannot know God's true nature.

"Yes, that's right. We're only going to get a glimpse of who God is."

I find that some people are actually missing the point by trying to understand certain concepts, like God, by obtaining some kind of proof. Can it be proven?

"There is a long history of arguments demonstrate that God exists, including the arguments of St. Anselm based on ontological considerations and St. Thomas Aquinas who uses cosmological arguments. These arguments can make a person believe in God."

I think sometimes philosophies can provide us with a better understanding of certain concepts. I wonder: Can a mystic be a philosopher or a philosopher a mystic?

"I think philosophers can be mystics just as all kinds of people can be mystics. What is a mystic and what does mystical mean? So in the Catholic tradition you can have a philosopher who has some kind of direct experience and knowledge of God."

"Then you may ask but how do you have such an experience? Usually it would be through prayer, the centre of the mystic experience."

So does this imply that anyone can be a mystic? If the way to explore mysticism is through prayer—well, anybody can pray. So do we all have the capacity to get into that realm through practice?

"Yes, it would imply that. There are many different types of prayer, prayers of asking, and prayers of thanksgiving but the mystical experience of people in Catholic tradition usually reach a state of prayer that does not use words, they enter a realm where they can just contemplate the divine without words. It is another level of connection with the divine."

Who was the Bible written for?

"Well, first of all we might need to clarify what constitutes the "bible" for different religious traditions. The Christian Old Testament and the Hebrew Scriptures for example not to mention difference between Christian traditions. But Christians would hold that the bible is destined for all humankind."

Do you think the Bible is still relevant?

"If you are not a believer you could still argue that the bible is relevant as a window into history and culture and religions. You might even argue that it lists basic human insights into what constitutes good moral behavior such as not killing, stealing and lying. The New Testament speaks of forgiveness, compassion, love and service and all these are good for society. But if you believe it is the word of God then it takes on a different dimension. It is not just a source of a moral code, it reveals who God is and what sort of relationship humans should have with their God."

How is mysticism perceived and practiced in Christianity?

"I think if you ask most Christians about mysticism they would be a little confused and certainly would not see themselves as mystics. Mysticism is for certain saints and for people with extraordinary gifts and experiences. Yet on further reflection we have all had times when God seem very close, or seems to be directing us and inspiring us through prayer and life's experiences."

Do you think there are different levels of mystical awareness?

"Yes, I suspect you are right. St. Teresa of Avila wrote a work called *The Interior Castle*, she was a mystic herself. The image is a castle, some people stand outside the gates of the castle, some enter the gates and some go into the various chambers, outer and inner of the castle. St Teresa uses the image to illustrate the stages of her spiritual life. Many just stay at the gates of prayer and the mystical life and others go right in there."

Can anybody really be like Jesus?

"Yes, I think that is the call of the Christian life. Jesus instructs his followers to love each other as He had loved them. The Eastern theological tradition places emphasis on the idea of the deification of humans, that is we become more like the divine and we share in the divine. We are not going to be Jesus strictly speaking because we are humans and we are not God."

But if we separate Christ's human nature and divine nature, can we be like him, or is He just this guy who founded a university that no one has ever graduated from? Because Christ really suffered as a man.

"If you believe that you are made in the image of God, and that Jesus came as a model of being fully human then yes, we can be like Him. Saints in the Christian tradition are examples of this."

Are Islam, Judaism and Christianity the same in some ways?

"Islam, Judaism and Christianity are all monotheistic and they come from a common regions of the world. They are also religions of the book. There are shared insights but also important differences. Obviously, a monotheistic religions have more in common with each other than with religions which are polytheistic, with many gods. Unfortunately, the similarities between the three have not stopped conflicts in the past and present."

CHAPTER 11

ALEX:
Conversation with a Professor of Psychology

How do you view the relationship between God and man? What do you think religion is for?

"I think that the different religions of the world are actually just different expressions of a much more fundamental thing, which is the spiritual nature of human beings. As we may see it, the different religions are actually the politics of the spirit. We're all looking for that which is fundamental, which is outside the physical world. It's what makes us tick.

"That's why psychology and spirituality are one and the same thing. In psychology we talk about behavior. We talk about the mind, but we're actually talking about that search we're all pursuing for meaning and understanding of life and the universe."

Can we explain our religious inclinations according to our backgrounds and comfort zones?

"Oh yes, I'm sure. As a psychologist, I'd have to say I'm aware all the time that people are keeping themselves within their comfort zone. We tend not to step out too much from that which is familiar and that which is shared by other people.

'In the work that I've done with refugees there's been an enormous amount of discomfort in entering a new community, particularly if that community has a different way of expressing spirituality and how it is expressed among other things in the law, how we regard human beings, their behavior, what's punishable and what's not. These all become focal points of discomfort."

How would you explain mysticism?

"Two words we use when we're talking about mysticism provide the building blocks of the human spirit. One is what we call the *cataphatic*; the other is the *apophatic*.

"The cataphatic vehicle brings us to an understanding of our spirituality through doctrines and teachings. It comes from devotion and devotional practices like prayer, worship, and the sacraments.

"That's very different from the apophatic, the search of meaning and the search for a God that is performed through that individuality that's right inside yourself."

Is the cataphatic approach a form of prayer?

"It can be, but it's also about rituals, sacraments, and writing and reading. A good example would be Islam. On the one extreme you've got the cataphatic Islamists who actually get all their understanding of God through the Quran and through the teachings of Mohammed. On the other end of the spectrum, you've got the apophatic, who are searching within themselves.

"In Christianity, you've got St. John of the Cross. He experienced God largely through his own direct links and understandings, not through anyone else's teachings."

Can you further explain St. John of God? He actually pointed out that any form of talking about God is far removed from God.

"That's right. In fact, the word we usually use about the mystical experience is 'ineffable,' which means something is too great or beautiful to be described or expressed. You experience it for yourself, sometimes even lacking words or images for that experience."

Is Christianity more cataphatic?

"It depends where you're coming from. The majority of Christians I know have probably come to their Christianity and maintained their Christianity through external things like taking part in public prayer and taking part in singing and so on. I do know some profoundly deep Christians who don't relate to any church because none of the rituals mean anything to them. What means something to them is their direct line with God. Often they are regarded as the oddball."

Who were the Bible and the Quran written for?

"All religious writings have evolved over a long period of time. For instance, what's in the Bible depends a great deal on what your religion is, because the Bible is interpreted very differently by Jews than it is by Christians.

"I think the Bible, in whichever form, was written for a specific community—for the political community that one calls their church. I know that the Quran and the Bible are both regarded as sacred texts, just as there are many Indian sacred texts and so on. They are regarded as belonging to God. In a practical sense, they're all edited to fit with the teachings, with the dogmas."

How relevant is the Bible?

"As a psychologist, I would have to say it depends the nature of your path. If you're on a search for particular explanations, then there will be bits of the Quran, bits of the Bible, bits of the Bhagavad Gita, all of which will help you."

Then it would be useful for people to read a variety of sacred texts?

"Indeed. There are also the writings of people who are not particularly religious but who are looking at fundamental truths. There's an excellent book, if you can find a copy, called *God in All Worlds: An Anthology of Contemporary Spiritual Writing* [edited by Lucinda Vardey and published in the US by Pantheon in 1995], about the nature of human beings and their relationship to the world, the universe, and to God."

How is mysticism perceived in practicing Christianity or Islam?

"Almost all Western religions have their own mystics. Unfortunately, I think mysticism has been the victim of bad press. The late nineteenth century and early twentieth century was plagued by people who set themselves up as mystics, pretending to be from mystical Eastern sects. Many of them were not genuine mystics. They were charlatans who played on people's gullibility."

What constitutes "mystical" in Christianity?

"Christianity is a religion that is centered on the existence of a God, that's God with a capital G. It and other theistic religions link the mystical practices and the mystical search. It's about your direct communication with God. There are other religions that are not theistic, that don't have a God. Buddhism is a good example of a nontheistic spirituality. That is, its teachings embrace a search for ultimate reality within yourself as well as outside of you."

Is there a link between Christianity, Islam, Judaism, and Hinduism?

"Yes, at the spiritual end of course there is. They are all trying to find a pattern of meaning. What is the ultimate meaning? Who are we? Why are we here? How does the world exist? That's common to all searches, not just religious searches, but philosophical searches. On the other hand, I think there are also parallels.

"There's the very fact that Jews, Christians, and Muslims all share a common set of understandings through the Old Testament. That shows you there's a fundamental body of shared knowledge and understandings largely through shared history.

"The folktales, like Noah's flood, exist across many parts of the human race, including some of the primitive peoples of the Americas, who had no direct communication with either the East or the West. There are lots of common tales like God's demand on Abraham to sacrifice his son, an expression of trust and belief. These occur in lots of cultures.

"You can look at it two ways. You can be a cynic and say a religion has grown up from myths that are common to all human beings. Or, you can look at it much more fundamentally, and say religions are a codified way of understanding those things which are the searches that human beings have, like the search for guidance."

What is the relationship between spirituality and psychology?

"Well, I can only speak for myself as a particular kind of psychologist. What we call 'psychology,' which derives from the Greek word 'psyche,' has come to mean the mind and behavior in modern psychology. In the original Greek, it means the soul. It's that intangible thing that makes us unique within the material world. But not all psychologists would give you the same answer. Many might even deny the existence of a spiritual 'self.'"

How relevant are religions and spirituality today?

"They're more relevant to some people than others. The more materially prosperous we become, the easier it is to find explanations of the meaning in the world, in the material and the tangible, and as a result we search less for it in the personal, the interpersonal, and the spiritual."

How is mysticism understood by modern psychology?

"I think it depends who you read. Most social psychologists don't really look at the concept of mysticism at all. They look at the organization of religion. They look at how it is a social phenomenon, how it supports and helps, how it develops ethical standards and so on. I am a cultural psychologist and I tend to look at the personal power of mysticism rather than its social effects."

CHAPTER 12

How I Met My Wife: Creating and Preserving Lasting Relationships

I had promised to tell Grace about my wife and how we met, but had not yet gotten around to it. While driving in to my office, our conversation turned to couples counseling and that afforded just the right opportunity.

"When I meet couples in my practice, they are either coming at the right time for couples counseling therapy or they've waited 'til it's too late. Usually there is one partner who wants to stay in the relationship more than the other. The trick is to guide them to a place where they both want the same thing—hopefully to stay in their current relationship. Regardless of how much or how little time they've spent building their relationship, they are typically lost in understanding how to effectively communicate with each other. The formula for a successful relationship is simple enough, but most couples never took the time to investigate.

"Couples tend to forget what it was like when they first met each other and fell in love—the infatuation, the passion, the unconditional love they shared. There was nothing they wouldn't do for each other, and that's the highest form of love, unconditional love, meaning, 'I give you more, even if it compromises my own comfort.' The beginning of love is always the most precious time of all. All of my clients have their beautiful stories to tell. And when they start relating their story of the unconditional love they once felt, the smiles return to their faces."

"I bet you have your own 'story to tell'—about how you met your wife," Grace hinted.

Remembering my promise, I replied, "Oh yes, I do!"

"How did you two meet? Was it romantic? What were the circumstances?" Grace asked.

"I must admit it happened quite by accident, pure luck," I replied. "And yes, you could call it romantic or perhaps even mystical, almost like a fairy tale. I fact, there was a moment when simply catching a train made all the difference—our fate hung in the balance. We think that such connections are random accidents, but when you look back from the perspective of time, you can see that there are no 'accidents'!

"So let me tell you the story ..."

As I pulled in to the office parking lot, I suggested we walk to a nearby park. It was a tranquil spot with a pond where black swans like to bathe. We found a bench and I began.

"We met in high school. I remember that my teacher asked me the year before if I had a steady girlfriend. I told her I had been going out with this girl for four months now, so I thought it was pretty serious. She laughed. At that time I didn't understand why would she laugh. I was very serious about my girl and the four months of dating seemed quite a commitment for a seventeen-year-old boy who was interested in nearly every girl that walked by.

"Little did I know that I would be dating her for another four years, and that she would become my wife, the mother of my children, and my best friend. She would even accompany me on my journey to the other side of the world!" I exclaimed with pride.

"She was certainly different from the rest. My attraction to Vera was sparked in an unusual way, I met her through a photograph."

"What do you mean, you 'met her through a photograph'?" Grace asked.

"Well, I had actually known Vera for few years. We had mutual friends, so we would meet each other at parties and such. We were just friends. She was also a close friend of my niece, Rena—they were classmates. And because Rena was more like a sister to me, we would often hang out together. I was living with my stepmother in the city at the time and since there was no love lost between us, I spent my weekends at my sister's house in a small town nearby.

"One day I was chatting with Rena about parties, who's going out with whom—you know, the typical teenage stuff—and she pulled out a recent photograph of Vera to show me. I hadn't seen Vera for at least a year. I remembered her as a freckle-faced kid, definitely not 'girlfriend material'," I said with a broad smile.

"But now I was seeing someone completely different. She was now a young lady, and a very good-looking one at that! What immediately captivated me were her eyes—so expressive that they seemed to be alive, as if they were popping out of the photo. It was only a black and white, head and shoulders shot, but she looked very glamorous and, yes, even sexy. I couldn't take my eyes of the photograph; I was spellbound. I told Rena that I wanted to get reacquainted with Vera and that she had to help me arrange it. Rena was a bit surprised by my ardor, and she said, 'OK, we're going to the market next Tuesday, why don't you come with us?' But she added, 'I can't guarantee that Vera will go.' And I told her, 'You have to *make* her go, no matter what!'

"This 'market' was more like a flea market, where people would bring unwanted household goods and clothing to sell. Really it was as much a social event as anything. So the day was set," I continued. "I didn't know if Vera would even come, but I was determined to go after her.

"I packed up some old clothes to sell in two large briefcases, and when the day arrived, I headed off to catch the morning train. I was running a little late, so I hightailed it to the station. As I approached the tracks near the station, the guardrails were already coming down signaling that the train was coming! I was still two kilometers from the train station, so I ran as fast as I could. The train stopped, then started to move again. My jacket was wide open and the two cases I was carrying were practically flying in the air. Though the train paused momentarily, I certainly didn't! I ran along side the train for all I was worth. I knew that it was my only chance; I felt that if I didn't catch that train, I might never see Vera again. In those days when there were no mobile phones, no social media—no Internet. It was summer vacation, and kids were often scattered everywhere and hard to track down. If I didn't reconnect with Vera now, who knows when I might get another chance? So I felt a sense of urgency. I was chasing my future, my destiny.

"As the train was entering the station I was still fifty meters behind. The train stopped to allow passengers to disembark and new passengers to board. I knew this wouldn't last long, so I ran even faster. Just as I reached the station, totally blown, the train started to move.

"I sprinted down the platform and drew alongside the last carriage of the departing the train. So I'm running alongside it now, and I catch one of the vertical bar handles and open the door. I heaved my cases inside the train, one by one. *Phew!* I knew I only had one chance to jump aboard that train. So, I stretched my body to get a grip on the door handle. *Yes!* I caught hold and gripping hard, and with my last bit of energy, I threw myself onto the step and into the carriage. I made it! Another second and my two briefcases would have left on that train without me.

"Wow!" Grace exclaimed, "You could have been killed if you'd fallen under the train!"

"Well, tell be honest, that never crossed my mind," I said sheepishly. "It just goes to show that if you want something badly enough, you'll do just about anything to get it. In my mind, failing was not an option."

"So what happened next?" Grace asked.

"I arrived about a half-hour later. I took my luggage and headed straight to the market. At first I didn't see any familiar faces. As I was poking through the stalls, I looked up and there she was. She was even more beautiful in real life. She was standing with a group of her friends, so I walked up and said as casually as I could manage, 'Oh hi, what are you doing here?' I put my sale items out next to hers and did my best to charm her with humor. I spent the next several hours chatting her up, so I didn't pay much attention to selling my stuff. At the end of the day, we gathered up our unsold items and Vera started to head for the train home.

"I said goodbye to her before she left. I knew I had to catch the same train so I could ask her for a date. As soon as she rounded the corner of the market on her way to the station, I handed my two briefcases to my friends and told them that they could sell the stuff and keep the money. I was a man possessed!

"Then I ran to the station to catch her up. I caught the train and found a seat near Vera and her friends. I told her how amazing it was that we 'accidentally' met today and said that surely such synchronicity couldn't be a coincidence. I don't think she guessed that I had engineered the whole thing.

"When we got back to the city, I offered to walk her home and she agreed. I was overjoyed. We walked slowly toward her home as the snow started to fall. It was all quite magical! When we got to her gate, our hair was covered in snowflakes. She asked, 'Would you like to come upstairs for a cup of tea?' Are you kidding? Of course, I said yes. I met her mother and one of her brothers, and the apartment was warm and cozy. It made me feel welcome and protected."

"How truly romantic!" Grace asserted.

"Yes, definitely mystical moments," I added nostalgically.

"Vera brought me a bowl of pea soup with a large sausage. I was surprised by her kindness and very, very happy," I said. "We listened to records for a while and then as I was leaving, she gave me a kiss on a cheek and sent me on my way. I was in heaven! I asked if she would like to meet me the next day and go to the nearest café. To my delight, she said yes.

Glancing at my watch, I exclaimed, "Oh, look at the time! Shall we go back?"

"That's a wonderful story. Can I use it in my assignment as a case study?" Grace inquired.

"Yes, of course. Ooh, I've really got to run, can we meet again next week?" I asked as I stood to leave.

"By all means," Grace affirmed.

Assessment

When was the last time you reflected on those wonderful days that lead to the formation of your most significant relationship? Do you remember the thrill of meeting the person that you fell in love with? Can you recall the unfolding miracle of love coming your way? How did you feel? Did your love at first feel like a runaway train? You were on your best behavior, you were witty and kind and considerate, and you'd do anything to protect your loved one. Your partner bared body, mind, and spirit to you. The intense intimacy that followed solidified your burning desire for one another. You wanted to be together all the time. You swore you'd be together forever and nothing could prevent you from traveling together into eternity.

Perhaps you got married and made plans for a family and a future filled with bliss. But as the years passed, your passion began to wane and your focus shifted to the children, your career, your bills, and so on. Your love seems to have lost momentum. The excuses mounted: *work is so demanding, there just isn't enough time to do it all. The children are wearing me out. How are we going to afford to send them to college?* Consequently, intimacy deteriorated and you started slowly drifting apart.

This is the perfect time to reflect on your relationship. It's like the changing of seasons. The season of passionate love is replaced by a season of occasional sex that serves more as a stress reducer than an expression of the love you once shared. Years pass all too quickly and the shift in focus from the passion of unconditional love to an obligatory kind of occasional lovemaking makes the whole business seem more like a chore than something to enjoy and look forward to. You are on the road to self-inflicted perdition. The arguments become more frequent and more heated, and you are both looking for a quick solution for this self-inflicted pain. Your relationship seems to deteriorate faster each day. You start thinking about an exit strategy, you've had enough ... *STOP!* You can see where this is heading.

Rewind. Only few years ago you couldn't live without each other, you would do anything for one another regardless of the price; you would have laid your life on the line in a heartbeat. Step back. Take a time-out. Bring her flowers and two tickets to a movie. Surprise him with a candlelight dinner. Book a short holiday. Turn off the electronic devices and send the kids to nana for the weekend. Get back to basics. Rekindle your relationship *now*.

Recall what your partner really liked when you first met. You knew his favorite song, her favorite flowers. Did she need your protection and your presence? Did he like your touch and loving connection? What happened to love?

While you might not have given it much thought, there are three main types of love:

Baby love

This type of love is self-centered pursuit in which everything revolves around one person only: "I can't be happy until you meet all my demands, and I will make your life miserable if I don't get what I want." In this case, "love" is mistaken for "power and control."

Exchange love

This is a quid quo pro arrangement: "I will only love you if I get something in return. I will be a good and loving partner, however, you need to treat me to 'X' first." This can be likened to a business transaction rather than a meaningful relationship.

Unconditional love

In this type of love, both partners display willingness to give freely to each other without consideration to their own comfort or needs. Understanding what the other person needs and knowing how to supply it is crucial. It's the kind of love that is displayed by new lovers early in a relationship, when nothing seems too difficult, and they complement other perfectly. Another example of this natural kind of love is demonstrated by the parents' love for their children.

Unconditional love is the highest form of relationship between two people. Unconditional love fulfills our highest of all needs—the need for *contribution*—giving beyond our own comfort zone, truly giving. The biblical injunction to "love your neighbor as yourself" encapsulates this higher form of love that is based on selfless contribution toward one another. Anyone can do this. All you need is to refocus, put emotions back into this relationship with renewed intimacy time, and form a new meaning. *You can do this*

CHAPTER 13

Closing the Circle

This time tomorrow, I will be in Japan.

"I wish you could stay longer," Grace said with sadness in her eyes. I wished I didn't have to go so soon, too.

"I'll be back again. You know I can't stay away from you for too long," I responded with a smile. "I hope you got some answers to your research questions."

"Yes, thanks to you I've got plenty of material to work with. I think I asked you enough questions and your narrative won't need much editing. I've got everything I need. "Perhaps it wouldn't hurt to recap the key points," Grace added.

"Yes, of course," I agreed.

"We started at reflecting on what makes our relationships more or less successful. Some of the new knowledge in biology such as epigenetics and quantum physics, gives us a better understanding of how our world is designed and what impact it has on the most fundamental building block of society—relationships. Everything in the universe is either cooperating or dying. The old premise that competition drives nature seems false. The better the relationship, the more the respective entities thrive—from subatomic particles to the larger universal design of planets, solar systems, and galaxies. Everything supports each other. Every living thing needs to cooperate. Plants need water and sunshine and exchange carbon dioxide for oxygen, animals cooperate to promote the survival of their species, and some of them form incredible social systems, like bees and ants. We humans are no exception; we must cooperate to protect our earthly environment or perish. The reason we're living in a world of conflict—with nature and each other—is the old system of competition, aggression, domination, and greed.

"The new world is in our hands: we can cooperate and work as one or perish. It's our choice; we are living in the most crucial moment in our evolutionary history. We became masters of our own destiny. We have gathered enough information to make an informed decision. How we arrange it is up to us."

"I am really fascinated by the links you make between science and the mystical," Grace interjected. "It seems so naturally logical, I don't understand why educating people about the new approaches and discoveries in science that demystify the true nature of the world we live in is such a slow process."

"I don't know why the process is so slow either, however, I can imagine that if you would have spent your entire life preaching that the world is flat and suddenly someone comes along with proof that it's actually round, you would probably be fearful of having your beliefs invalidated. Some people embrace change while others resist. Of course not all new ideas are necessarily true, but when idea is closely examined and tested and the new proposition turns out to be true, the motive for continued resistance becomes suspect. There are many historical examples; the powerful institutions don't give up their influence easily. When Copernicus demonstrated that the sun is at the center of our solar system and the Earth is only one of many planets orbiting it, the Church would not change its position on the subject. It was theologically and practically too risky to suddenly tell people that the Church's teachings had been wrong for fifteen hundred years. Its authority was threatened therefore its sphere of influence diminished, which in the end also means lost revenue."

"Yes, there seems to always be someone in charge who wants to rule the world!" Grace laughed.

"Well you aren't far off, Grace. In whose interest is it nowadays to withhold information from the public or misinform them on scientifically proven discoveries?"

"Big Pharma comes to mind," she responded without hesitation.

"Yes, I agree. They sell billions of dollars worth of drugs and do not want any interruptions in their attempts to control the population. This is not some kind of conspiracy theory; today, many people are aware that drugs—especially the psychotropic medications that are supposed to help people feel more mentally stable—are being overprescribed. As a consequence, many patients get hooked on drugs that do more damage than good."

"I think I know what you mean; epigenetics biology is a good example," said Grace. "We've talked about the fundamental discrepancy in understanding about how the trillions of body cells actually work. I'm not a biologist, still it's not difficult for me to understand that the environment, and not the genetics or heredity, that is the key to well-being. If we place cells in crystal clear water, they will naturally function better than those submerged in diesel!" Grace said with her eyes opened wide in amusement.

"That's for sure, Grace. The environment is the key—it gives us the choice to succeed, as opposed to being a victim of our ancestry. Epigenetics places the driving brain on the *outside* of the cell as opposed to the old biology that insisted it was inside in the nucleus. Interestingly, many biologists didn't make the connection that our brains develop the same building blocks from our epidermis as those that create the cell's membrane—the part that drives the cell. Incidentally, we might also make the connection between the non-local consciousness that is also not inside our brains, but on the outside, translating waves from the frequency domain into our thoughts and projected perceptions. If this is all true—and the new science confirms that it is—there should be no need for psychotropic drugs.

"Keep in mind, the pharmaceutical companies had an interest in the Human Genome Project that attempted to map all the genes in the human body. The project needed to identify at least a hundred thousand genes to conduct the experiment, based on the assumption that if there are a hundred thousand enzymes (for example, the proteins that generate complex reactions in gene cells), there must be at least a hundred thousand genes. No so. Embarrassingly, they found that only twenty-three thousand genes make up a human person—an amount similar to that of a small roundworm (*Caenorhabditis elegans*) that has only 1,271 cells in its entire body—the human person comprises a trillion cells! How can this be? HGP Scientists expected and wrongly assumed that the more complex organisms must possess a greater number of genes.

"Their objective was to promote the project as a humanitarian endeavor, however, the real outcome they expected was to sell the information for use in identifying drugs, from which they anticipated reaping gigantic profits. The failure of finding one hundred thousand genes led to the new discovery that our genes are not self-arising. Unfortunately a large sector of the public still believes in genetic determinism.

"So the Human Genome Project failed miserably. And thank God for that. Otherwise, if all the genes had been identified, it would open the possibility that all the human genes can be mapped and separated for the good ones and those potentially future disease-carrying ones. For those disease-carrying ones, pharmaceutical companies would develop drugs to control the problem. The upshot would be that every person would be diagnosed for future ailments even before they were born and they would receive 'appropriate medications.' Can you imagine what kind of society we would become? Enslaved and at the mercy of the drug companies."

"I hadn't thought of it like that. Wow! That's a horrific scenario!" Grace exclaimed. "In the face of this level of control, the church-sponsored Spanish Inquisition seems tame by comparison," she added with concern.

"Isn't the whole failure of the genome project a bit mystical? When the greed for control was about to descend on humanity, something incredible happened. Unexpectedly, it was revealed to the scientists that the nature of our bodies is not so predictable. Sometimes I imagine that when God was creating life on Earth, He must have predicted the possibility that humans might deduce that they can gain control in this way, so when scientists came close to solving the genetic riddle, they found more questions than answers," Grace flashed a smile.

"I am fascinated by your exploration of the mystical," she continued. "Now I understand what it means to be a 'mystic'. It's a new way of looking at the same things, but from a different point of view."

"Yes, it's like being in a room and moving to a different corner. It's the same room, but from each corner the room looks different. It's just a matter of perspective—the way we look at things makes them change as we look at them.

"Similarly, to experience the mystical one must fulfill certain conditions. It's just like water or matter of any kind that we take for granted: once we investigate deeply, we realize that every molecule of water is made up of oxygen and hydrogen, and all matter is made of tiny elements of electrons and tiny quarks that drive the whole larger mechanism. Mysticism can only be experienced by focusing on this possibility and then practicing it. Aristotle reminds us that we become what we repeatedly do; therefore, happiness is not an act but a habit.

"Brian Tracy teaches a similar approach when he says that if you have to be addicted to something—and we are all creatures of habit by our nature—then choose to become addicted to endorphins, the hormones in our brains that are responsible for making us feel happy. He instructs that by repeating behaviors practiced by successful, happy people, you will become like them—successful and happy."

Grace reflected, "This sounds so simple, yet somehow so difficult to accomplish." Why is it so hard for us to be sustainably happy?"

"It's hard to know how other people experience reality. Most people know what *should* be done, just as they know the difference between good and bad, but they don't know *how* to do it. It's like having a pin number for the ATM machine that accesses your 'happiness bank.' While you have the required four digits, they won't work if they are out of sequence. No matter how hard you try, you will not be able to tap into your 'happiness account.' Worse still, if you try too many times, the bank will confiscate your card! Think of each number representing a concept: the first pin number might represent Self-Awareness (1), the second, Meaning (2), the third, Focus (3), and the fourth, Perseverance (4). So the correct sequence is 1, 2, 3, 4."

"Yes, I can see it now," said Grace. "If you put perseverance first, and as a result of all your hard work, you find the meaning, and then you focus your energies, your self-awareness could be skewed or false. So if you have your sequence out of order, that combination won't open your happiness bank. You can wear yourself out with so much effort, but you're wasting your time and going nowhere."

"You got it." I confirmed.

Shifting subjects, Grace allowed, "My favorite story was the one about your mother's eyes. When you were telling me about this experience I felt like I was there with you. Thanks for showing me how to get into trance. Can anyone be self-hypnotized and going into trance at any time?"

"Yes, of course. Anybody can experience trance state, although some people are more susceptible than others. With practice, you can get increasingly better at it, as with any other routine. I highly recommend the practice of self-hypnosis, meditation, or similar practices that promote mindfulness and relaxation. I routinely offer self-hypnosis and deep relaxation techniques in my practice.

"Trance or dissociation is common in our everyday lives. If you've ever driven a car, you've been under trance; it's the temporary dissociation of the body and mind. Your body is driving your car—changing gears, checking mirrors, talking to someone, and being fully aware of the traffic at the same time. However, your mind might be elsewhere—thinking about your next holiday or how you're going to explain to your boss why you're late. You might drive a mile or two and then realize that you don't remember how you got there, you've been leaving your body to do the driving while you've being off somewhere else in your mind.

Trance state is like being in two places at the same time. In hypnosis, this phenomenon is used to go deeper and longer; to tap into the subconscious as the brain slows down into delta waves. This is similar to the relaxation you experience in sleep, but you are not sleeping. Thanks to this internal communication, you might find that you are able to recall memories that you haven't visited for a long time. This can assist in identifying and clearing out clogged mental passages that would otherwise remain blocked. Under deep trance, many people are able to dissociate themselves from negative thoughts or memories, or even chronic pain. I have seen clients who could not sit still without pain for more than thirty seconds, yet under trance they can sit quietly and calmly for an hour or more without complaint. They can have their eyes open or closed; they are fully aware, yet fully immersed in deep relaxation of the whole body under the directives of the mind.

"These stories are only examples of how rich are our lives are, how mystical is the whole creation of the human person. You have your own story to tell, Grace. You've been through a lot. The joys, disappointments, grieving losses, accomplishments, tests, and trials. We all have our share.

"If you reflect on your life, I know you would discover the tremendous richness of your life experience, and if your shared that with others, it would encourage them to bring their stories out into the light. Sometimes we think that other people are important and their lives are so interesting, but we often forget that each one of us have equal potential to enrich other people's lives. We contribute and influence others continually; sometimes they will tell us and thank us for it, but usually we would never know. Just by sharing stories, we may trigger something in someone's heart or mind that can have long-lasting consequences.
"I just heard about a person I met several years ago. At that time she was at a crossroads, very confused and not knowing what to do next. We didn't know each other well; she was my wife's former work colleague. I met her once over coffee as my wife and I were on our way to Tasmania. She asked how I made the shift from the

disaster of losing everything to influencing others. I told her about my experiences and encouraged her to go back to her studies and reinvent herself. Only few days ago I learned that following our conversation she enrolled in a graduate program and is now a practicing counselor and psychotherapist in Switzerland. She is helping and influencing many people in need; thanks to her new skills, her clients are forming better relationships and becoming better functioning persons. And it all started by us chatting over cup of coffee!

"Everything in the universe has a purpose. There are no meaningless coincidences just attractions. Consciousness is the factor that is causing the exchange of these energies. From collaborations between tiny particles of vibrating energy to galactic exchanges—it's all linked by the same golden tread of non-local consciousness. Our brains are merely receivers tuned to the frequencies that the brain processes into concepts that we can understand. The better the quality of the receiver, the better the quality of its projected perception. Your energy will follow whatever you focus on and, with persistence, turn it into emotions that will give you the result you want.

"If meaning is the key to a happy life, how can we find the meaning that is aligned uniquely for each of us? Most people would want to find meaning by becoming healthy, attractive, wealthy, and educated. Most of us know what we want but sometimes we don't know how to get it. What if that elusive sense of meaning was communicated through messages from the universal consciousness? No longer would we search for meaning from inside our heads; we would tune our mind's receivers to obtain messages of meaning from the non-local consciousness. It's as if we were living submerged in a deep ocean of that consciousness. We all live inside of it, but instead of tapping into its vastness of wisdom, some of us struggle with what we know or are used to in our heads—kind of like a fish swimming in the ocean denying that the sea water flowing through its body system is not the source of its life force."

"We could talk forever! There are so many other things I'd like to ask you about," Grace said, adding wistfully, "I wish you didn't have to go so soon."

"Actually I'll be coming back soon, you know. I don't think I told you that two of the local monasteries have invited me to collaborate with them on applying my research on mysticism to a new method of communication in schools."

Grace clapped her hands with childlike joy and exclaimed, "Excellent! Now let's grab your luggage and get going—the traffic to the airport is bound to be heavy this afternoon."

We jumped into her car and rolled out of her driveway. We had half an hour to get to airport. I completed my airline check-in on my phone. My passport was in my wallet. Tomorrow I would be in Tokyo talking with Zen monks. I was having mixed feelings: excited about my new project and feeling sad to leave Grace behind. She's been outstanding company, as always.

New Beginnings

Noted psychotherapy and counseling researcher Carl Rogers reminded us that relationship is a natural structural component of self-actualization. Science tells us that the drive for self-actualization is shared by the entire spectrum of life on our planet, and mysticism plays an important role in self-actualization. Those whose stories are profiled within these pages confirm the importance of all relationships, beginning with the one we have with ourselves and carrying on through to the union with God and all creation. Their thoughtful comments reveal that if the relationship is compromised, this natural, organic, and universal equilibrium is knocked out of balance, and this can lead to conflict and unhappiness. However, when the relationship becomes deeper and more meaningful, it reaches another level that taps into the realm of mysticism. In this context, my interviewees agreed that we all share this capacity—*we are all mystics.*

Modern counseling stresses the importance of a meaningful relationship as a fundamental element of our quest for happiness, but my research ventures beyond this conventional trope by revealing that the heightened level of awareness in a relationship can pave the way for mystical experiences—beginning in therapeutic collaboration and continuing well beyond. Mysticism can only be experienced firsthand; it is all about personal perception.

This isn't some New Age psychobabble—as we've discovered, science and mysticism are really only opposite sides of the same coin; they complement each other as *yin* is to *yang*. Both are aimed at searching for meaning and better ways for people to flourish in their personal quest for happiness

As we have seen, mystical experiences are likely much more prevalent than reported. We have also witnessed the profound role mysticism can play in a holistic approach to counseling. I hope you will give mysticism a try. You already have the means—it is your birthright—you need only learn the way. You, too, can become a self-actualized Modern Mystic. *Seek and ye shall find ...*

Acknowledgements

This book is my personal statement based on my experience as a psychotherapist and beyond however, without support of my family, friends and associates this book would not come alive. Therefore, I would like to thank all the people who in many ways contributed to this project.

First and foremost I would like to thank my family:

Karolina and Jan Kanik for falling in love and having me without which this book would have never been written

Olga and Boleslaw Dziki, my in-laws, for their invaluable contribution and assistance over many years

Ian and Kasia – for awakening the mystical reality in me upon their arrival, and their uninhibited love, the two most precious souls who call me dad

Viesia – My wife the greatest source of love and support, my friend and my soulmate, my passionate guide, for your encouragement, believing in me, caring and shielding me, for your inspiration, your patience, wholehearted commitment, and your everlasting love, this project would not be possible without your unreserved care and thoughtfulness

Krystyna Lis, Jadzia Stachura, Andrzej Kanik Wieslaw Kanik my dearest sisters and brothers for their motivations and wisdom passed on to me despite being separated by many mountains and oceans

Mirek Lis, my nephew for his affectionate beautiful friendship that was cut short and our mystical encounters that followed

Wawrzyniec Kanik, my grandfather, for his continuous inspiration to carry on the mission ever since he stepped on the American soil over 100 years ago

Wladyslaw and Emilia Kanik, my uncle and aunty for their kind and unreserved support during my youthful forming years

My close friends and mentors whose kind presence made this project conceivable:

(in alphabetical order)

Prof Peter Black, for his kind friendship, invaluable insights and spiritual guidance

Dr Gerald Corey for his outstanding professional guidance and friendship, for being the first to suggest that there could be a book in me during our walks on the streets of San Francisco

Dr Richard Hamilton, for his friendship and invaluable time spent together while examining multitude of philosophical visions

Dr Mostafa Ismail for sharing his deep cultural insights bigheartedly

John Paul II, for reminding me "do not be afraid" and then

motivate to "what's possible"

John Lennon, for turning me on all those years ago

Cloe Madanes, for sharing her invaluable professional knowledge, her guidance and introducing me to persons of superior healing consciousness

Prof Alex Main for his generosity with time and content and introducing me to new concepts

Fr. Anscar McPhee for his friendship and opening my eyes to an exceptional new view of reality

Prof Martin Philpott for being the first in encouraging me to pursue academic research into mysticism in therapy

Dr Neil Preston for his kind friendship and invaluable time spent together on deep reflective conversations that resulted in derived guidance

Tony Robbins, for his outstanding generosity expressed so kindly to me and my wife, for inspiration to re-ignite my desire to unleash the power in me

Rev. Joseph Walsh, for his encouragement to express my spirituality through means of visual arts and hands on participation in the local community

Dr Michael Yapko for his deep insight and encouragement to pursue a lifetime of great hypnotic experience mystical or otherwise

Editors

Kim Cousins for her enthusiasm and conscientious application at the initial editing stages

Aden Nichols for his authentic insightful and outstanding final editing work

Designers

Ian Kanik for his discerning and heartfelt design consultations

Kasia (Catherine) Kanik for her most creative visual concepts in crafting of this book cover

Robert McManus for his exceptional graphic design skills at the final stages of creating this book's cover

Coaches

Jill Cheeks for her invaluable contribution and exceptional guidance in the final stages in creating of this book

Lauren Sullivan for her outstanding mentoring assistance at the crucial stages in the beginnings of this book project

Julie-Ann Harper and her team at Pick a WooWoo Publishing Group for an outstanding support throughout the crucial stages of assembling this book project into cohesive final form

Friends

Gerry and Lucy Gier for their extraordinary friendship resulted in sharing together many beautiful moments over many years

John Douglass, for his outstanding friendship, assistance and inspiration

Dr Gosia and Peter Mazur for their exceptional friendship and encouragement

Peter Urbanke, for his lifelong infrangible friendship and his encouragement

Moira Wright, for her unique friendship and support, kindheartedness and inspiration

and

My professional colleagues and associates for "holding the hope"

My past, present and future Clients, for continuously inspiring my interest in mysticism

It is not possible to name you all. You know who you are, who helped me to give birth to this book. I thank you all from the bottom of my heart.